Kyle Winkler makes one of [the activation of God's Wo...] resource will change your life, family, and destiny!

—Sid Roth

Host, *It's Supernatural!*

The Bible is the ultimate success handbook, and it requires an activation step—speak. The key to living a victorious life in Christ is, without a doubt, speaking the Word. *Activating the Power of God's Word* sets you up to succeed by giving practical directives.

—Marilyn Hickey

President and Founder, Marilyn Hickey Ministries

Kyle has done it again! This book is a must-have, practical tool for young and old alike that will literally transform your life! It is revelatory and biblically sound. He proves that just one word from God can change your life forever!

—Bishop Dale C. Bronner, DMin

Founder/Senior Pastor, Word of Faith

Family Worship Cathedral

One of the best ways to combat the schemes of the enemy is to boldly pray the Word of God, because when we stand on the truth of the Lord, the enemy must flee. Kyle's new book, *Activating the Power of God's Word*, will help you make the most of the living and active Word of God in your everyday life.

—Tom Mullins

Founding Pastor, Christ Fellowship

If you've ever wondered how your Bible heroes landed in the Hall of Faith, you need to read Kyle Winkler's new book. In *Activating the Power of God's Word* Kyle reveals a fresh revelation on the power of the spoken Word and offers practical examples. The declarations within these pages will build your faith in who God says you are and what you can do in His name. Whether you're facing battles or walking in victory, this book will encourage you to press into new dimensions of breakthrough in your life.

—Jennifer LeClaire
Senior Editor, *Charisma* magazine
Director, Awakening House of Prayer
Author, *Mornings With the Holy Spirit*

Words are powerful! They can either give life or bring death, yet many believers are ignorant of the power they possess in their own mouths to bring change and transformation to the world around them. In his latest book Kyle Winkler takes the believer on a journey to discover the supernatural power of declaration. In *Activating the Power of God's Word* you will receive biblical keys from the Word of God to make strategic declarations that will bring the change that you deeply desire. This is -more than a book; it is a manual for supernatural breakthrough.

—Kynan Bridges
Author, *Unmasking the Accuser*
Senior Pastor, Grace & Peace Global Fellowship
Host, *Life More Abundantly*

ACTIVATING
THE **POWER** OF
GOD'S
WORD

ACTIVATING
THE **POWER** OF
GOD'S
WORD

KYLE WINKLER

CHARISMA
HOUSE

Most Charisma House Book Group products are available at special quantity discounts for bulk purchase for sales promotions, premiums, fundraising, and educational needs. For details, write Charisma House Book Group, 600 Rinehart Road, Lake Mary, Florida 32746, or telephone (407) 333-0600.

Activating the Power of God's Word by Kyle Winkler
Published by Charisma House
Charisma Media/Charisma House Book Group
600 Rinehart Road
Lake Mary, Florida 32746
www.charismahouse.com

Unless otherwise noted, all Scripture quotations are taken from the New Revised Standard Version of the Bible. Copyright © 1989 by the Division of Christian Education of the National Council of the Churches of Christ in the USA. Used by permission.

Scripture quotations marked esv are from the Holy Bible, English Standard Version. Copyright © 2001 by Crossway Bibles, a division of Good News Publishers. Used by permission.

Scripture quotations marked mev are from the Modern English Version. Copyright © 2014 by Military Bible Association. Used by permission. All rights reserved.

Scripture quotations marked nasb are from the New American Standard Bible, copyright © 1960, 1962, 1963, 1968, 1971, 1972, 1973, 1975, 1977, 1995 by The Lockman Foundation. Used by permission. (www.Lockman.org)

Scripture quotations marked nirv are from the New International Reader's Version®. Copyright © 1996, 1998 Biblica. All rights reserved throughout the world. Used by permission of Biblica.

Scripture quotations marked niv are taken from the Holy Bible, New International Version®, NIV®. Copyright © 1973, 1978, 1984, 2011 by Biblica, Inc.™ Used by permission of Zondervan. All rights reserved worldwide. www.zondervan.com. The "NIV" and "New International Version" are trademarks registered in the United States Patent and Trademark Office by Biblica, Inc.™

Scripture quotations marked nkjv are taken from the New King James Version®. Copyright © 1982 by Thomas Nelson. Used by permission. All rights reserved.

Cover design by Justin Evans

Visit the author's website at kylewinkler.org.

Library of Congress Cataloging-in-Publication Data:
An application to register this book for cataloging has been submitted to the Library of Congress.
International Standard Book Number: 978-1-62998-971-6
E-book ISBN: 978-1-62998-972-3

21 — 9 8 7 6 5 4 3 2
Printed in the United States of America

Visit the author's website at kylewinkler.org.

Library of Congress Cataloging-in-Publication Data
An application to register this book for cataloging has been submitted to the Library of Congress.

International Standard Book Number 978-1-62998-971-6
E-book ISBN 978-1-62998-972-3

While the author has made every effort to provide accurate telephone number and Internet addresses at the time of publication, neither the publisher nor the author assumes any responsibility for errors or for changes that occur after publication.

21 — 987654321
Printed in the United States of America.

To mentors in the faith:
Thank you for the path you've forged
and the wisdom you've imparted.
Your legacy lives on through the lives of those of us
who now run with your baton.

CONTENTS

Part Five: Strategic Declarations to Win Spiritual Battles

ACKNOWLEDGMENTS

I AM GRATEFUL TO Charisma House for your continued belief in me and for providing a tremendous platform to share what God has taught me. Special thanks to Maureen Eha for your advocacy of this project and Megan Turner for your work with my words.

Many thanks to my friends and family who have supported and interceded for me for so long. In particular, thanks to Dr. Leo Carney, a true brother in the Lord: thank you once again for all the time you so selflessly gave to review each chapter. Dr. Jim Harris: thank you for your ongoing mentorship, which has truly shaped me. Barbara Tapp: thank you for your years of coaching, which have undoubtedly helped to hone my writing.

And finally, to the partners of my ministry: thank you for your generosity and prayers. You share in the impact and blessings of this book.

INTRODUCTION

WOVEN INTO THE very foundation of creation is a law stronger than any of the laws of nature. It is a force that cannot be rivaled and is more dependable than gravity. It is a supernatural power that when tapped, radically transforms anything to which it is applied.

Consider the strength, courage, and awe-inspiring miracles of some of your favorite Bible heroes. What is the "active ingredient" that...

- God used to give structure to the creation?
- The psalmist found as the source of prosperity?
- David discovered is the key to strength and refreshment in the midst of difficulties?
- Jesus modeled as the method to resist Satan?
- Peter engaged to heal those who were crippled?
- Paul revealed is the way to live in victory?

Have I piqued your interest? The answer, though often overlooked, actually isn't all that hidden. It is the *spoken* Word of God.

In the beginning, when God created the heavens and the earth, the earth was formless and empty (Gen. 1:1–2). Then God spoke! The creation story reveals that the spoken Word of God—with a "Let there be..." thundering into the void—declared destiny to darkness and lit up the cosmos with purpose, meaning, and life.

This single moment established God's spoken Word as the linchpin of creation. This is what the author of Hebrews reveals.

He sustains all things by his powerful word.

—HEBREWS 1:3

Indeed, God's Word holds *all things* together. How awesome! God's spoken Word maintains the planets in their orbits and the seasons in their cycles. As we will review in chapter 1, God's Word is the bedrock bond at the cellular level, holding even our human bodies together.

We marvel at the grandeur of God's design and the sheer majesty of His power. But perhaps most remarkable is that God made this power accessible to common people such as you and me. His spoken Word wasn't just relegated to a special group some thousands of years ago. No, the spellbinding reality is that you—yes, you!—may activate the power of God's Word *today* to transform your life *forever*. And that is the purpose of this book: to build your confidence that God's Word spoken through your mouth will accomplish the same things it accomplished for your favorite Bible heroes. Through strategic declarations, you will learn how to activate God's Word just as they did to transform every area of your life.

The power of God's spoken Word declares destiny into whatever seems hopeless. It gives identity to that which seems empty or meaningless. It provides the strength you need to get through difficulties, leads you through dark valleys, and heals sickness. It is the basis by which you can overcome life's greatest obstacles and win in every battle. Finally, as you will soon discover—and experience—the power of God's spoken Word sustains you as "more than a conqueror" in the life of overwhelming victory that Jesus died to give you (Rom. 8:37).

From Timid to Tenacious

Today I speak boldly before thousands, and through media countless more hear my messages. But if you would have told me this in my childhood or teenage years, I might have shuddered in fear and broken out in a cold sweat. Certainly I wouldn't have believed it. I wasn't always this daring, you see. But I came to be as I am, not by sheer chance or by wishing, but by applying the principle of speaking God's Word and letting it do its work in my life.

I can't explain why, but I remember being afraid of just about everything as a child. Have you ever heard of someone who dropped out of preschool? Now you have! Even though the preschool was barely one block from our house, I just did not want to be there that first year. So I begged and pleaded with my mom until she agreed to pull me out. Yes, preschool dropout—that is me!

I didn't get any braver by elementary school. In kindergarten and first grade I was so timid that when called to read aloud, I would freeze and lower my head in embarrassment because I just couldn't continue. My teachers assumed I had a reading problem and needed more help, so the school authorities enrolled me in a group with six other students for more individualized attention. My parents were confused by this action because I could read just fine at home.

What my teachers didn't immediately discern is that I didn't have a reading problem; I had a timidity issue. When called on to read aloud, I was simply too shy and insecure to speak up. By second grade I came out of my shell a bit. When my teachers realized that I could actually read well, they promoted me from the "yellow finches," the lowest reading group, to the "bluebirds," the highest.

Friendships and social groups were already well established by second grade, and because my shyness had kept me from interacting with most of my classmates, I had few friends in those early years. And my social status definitely wasn't helped by my frequent fumbling of the ball while playing sports in PE class or at recess. So my identity was established in the eyes of my classmates, and possibly worse, it was cemented within me. I was the quiet kid. The reject. The loner. The wimp.

Perhaps you can relate in even a small way. We have all been teased and picked on to some degree. We have all faced some sort of rejection, whether chosen last for a team, "friend-zoned" by a crush, or overlooked for a job. These are realities of life.

But what can make these experiences debilitating is when they happen so often that they cloud the lenses through which you see your present and future. As we will examine in chapter 4, this is the devil's work. As the accuser he is always building a case of evidence against us to present as a reason to live in misery and defeat. He especially finds power in words by others from the past or former weaknesses or regrets.

This is how he shackled me for much too long. "You will always be shy," I was constantly led to believe. "You will always feel rejected." When thoughts such as these are at the foundation of a person's belief about himself, they influence his behaviors. I was no exception.

By the time I changed schools for ninth grade, I was so convinced that I would never fit in with the popular crowd that I was awkward anytime I spoke to someone within those circles. The rejection was self-perpetuating. I would be rejected because I expected to be rejected.

I will reveal more aspects of my story throughout this book. But suffice it to say, these personal issues of insecurity and identity plagued me well into my early adult years, causing me great doubts and fears while hindering my relationships.

Men and women of all ages reading this have stories similar to or even far worse than mine. But I come with great news! This book offers a pivotal moment and an opportunity to begin to transform everything about you today. That is the second half of my story.

The path to where I am today came through a mixture of teaching and revelation. I was blessed enough to begin my born-again Christian journey in a church that unashamedly boasts in the power of God's Word to impact life. We were taught the basic principles of placing our identity in Christ, believing Scripture instead of feelings, and trusting God for healing despite symptoms. To be sure, this teaching initiated a newfound confidence in me.

Still, "some things are taught, while others are *caught*." This means that for certain situations, teaching can take you only so far. Teaching is great for head knowledge and to build a foundation on, but sometimes real and lasting transformation happens only through a personal encounter—that is, through life situations leading you to "catch" the principles and then to apply them yourself. That is how the most decided change in me began.

Stand in Victory!

After an all-out onslaught against my mind, one that nearly talked me out of the ministry, I knew that my destiny depended on putting God's Word to work in my life. Knowing what the Bible says about who I am and what I have in Christ wasn't enough; I had to learn how to live in these truths.

The Holy Spirit led me to an "aha" moment when I caught the solution. I was studying the full armor of God in Ephesians 6 with the goal of exploring the historical functions of each of the six pieces as well as the practical application for contemporary Christianity. As I read the passage with fresh eyes, my attention focused on the word *stand*. "Be strong in the Lord and in the strength of his power," Paul began (Eph. 6:10). "Put on the whole armor of God, so that you may be able to *stand* against the wiles of the devil" (v. 11). As Paul continued to describe the armor, I counted at least two more instructions to "stand."

God used this to speak something profound that is now a theme of my ministry. He said, "Don't fight with a devil who is defeated, but stand in the victory of the One who defeated him." Perhaps you should reread that and digest it a bit. The implications of this revelation are enormous. Stand on the truths of God's Word regardless of how bleak the situation looks. Stand in who God says you are despite what others have said about you. Stand on the promises of what God says you have regardless of the obstacles in the way. Stand on the assurance that the victory won by Christ's finished work is also your victory.

More than giving just a catchy one-liner, God also instructed me about the way to actually do this. "*Take*...the sword of the Spirit, which is the word of God," He said (Eph. 6:17). Through my historical study of the Roman sword, I discovered that often the soldier stood firmly planted in his place, waving his sword at oncoming enemies. This was his way of warning, "Stay back! I'm armed and dangerous." I knew I had to take up God's Word in the same way. That is, I had to stand planted in the truth, consistently declaring it over my life and into my situations.

When I felt confronted with rejection or purposelessness, I needed to declare God's Word: "I am handpicked and chosen by God for His good purpose" (Eph. 1:4). Or when feeling weak: "The joy of the Lord is my strength" (Neh. 8:10). Or in temptation: "I resist the devil and he must flee from me" (James 4:7). God's Word provides truth for any situation we face. We will explore this more in chapter 3 so that you can activate the Word's power in your life.

A Download From God

God's Word is designed to be declared. We see precedents for this throughout the Old and New Testaments. While we aren't to use God's Word as if it is a magical formula, declaring it aloud does act as a healing salve. When applied, God's Word goes to work to accomplish whatever it is meant to accomplish—not always overnight, but over time.

So in time I began to see God's Word transform areas of my life. My boldness tremendously increased and so did my confidence. I recognized that God's spoken Word applied to my attitude kept me in joy when things were anything but joyful. And I instantly found it an effective way to ward off the temptations of the flesh.

But often for something to be effective, it has to be used

consistently. And the spoken Word of God is no different. Think of it as taking a vitamin for your health. Sure, a vitamin can help give an instant boost when you are feeling under the weather, but it works best if you take it before you are sick. When you take vitamins daily and proactively, your immune system remains built up to fight off any potential attacks before they arrive. In the same way I found that my sustained victory and growth depended on a consistent, daily habit of speaking God's Word, not an occasional emergency dose.

To bolster this habit of speaking God's Word, I tried to keep handwritten scriptures on note cards in my pocket to declare throughout the day. But too often I forgot them at home, or the day's distractions caused me to forget to pull them out. Frustrated, I finally murmured to the Lord, "There must be a way to put the Word of God in my pocket for quick access whenever and wherever I need it."

That is when the download happened. Almost instantly an idea formed in my mind for a smartphone app. And my techno-savvy brain shifted into overdrive with the concept and possibilities. Even the name of the app came quickly: Shut Up, Devil!

The basic concept was clear: identify a collection of common issues that we all face—issues such as anxiety, discouragement, fear, financial struggle, and temptation—and then select scriptures related to each one of these issues and present them on digital note cards. Each card was to feature the base scripture with a personalized version crafted to speak aloud. And that was crucial. This wasn't another one of the many Bible promise apps meant for meditation (as great as those are). No, this was to be a sword in the pocket to help people apply the power of God's Word to any issue they face. The final, significant requirement was that the app needed to include a reminder feature with alerts to help users stay proactive about the practice.

Months later this "download from God" launched with fanfare and great support from the church and Christian media. In fact, to date it has become one of the most popular apps of its kind. Perhaps you came to this book because of it. Or maybe you know nothing about it but would like to. (It is available free at www.shutupdevil.org.)

However you got here, this book isn't about the app, but about the practice now made popular by the app: speaking God's Word.

How to Use This Book

I have intended this book as one from which you learn *and* with which you interact. First, I want to build your confidence in the principle of speaking God's Word. That is what the first part explores. Through it you will begin to understand that God's Word is meant to be spoken and meant to be spoken by you. I want to help increase your faith so that when you declare God's Word, you are sure it will work to transform your life.

In the next four parts I have handpicked sixteen strategic declarations in four different areas that make up the totality of life: identity and purpose, rest and refreshment, overcoming obstacles, and winning spiritual battles. Each chapter, which represents a declaration, is filled with solid, biblical teaching and numerous supporting verses to inspire faith in and to support each declaration. Understand that these are not strings of words to flippantly mouth to get whatever you want. No, each declaration is a holy decree set apart by God, given to you to use to conform to His truths. Any other use is a perversion of God's intentions.

At the end of each chapter with a theme declaration, you will see #ActivateTheWord followed by a personalized declaration designed for you to speak aloud. The goal here is to help you identify with and then activate the truth presented. That is when real transformation begins. Feel free to share these declarations and your life change with your friends on social media.

Be expectant of the great change in you that is about to take place as you begin to activate the power of God's Word. My story of transformation is not unique. I have heard from many people throughout the world, some coming to me with tears in their eyes, about how speaking God's Word has changed them too. Some were rescued from the grips of suicidal thoughts, others from the shackles of despair, depression, or post-traumatic stress disorder (PTSD). One young man shared with me about how proclaiming God's Word gave him the confidence that he was good enough to go to college.

Each story is different, but each reflects a common truth that God's Word declared over any situation will absolutely transform it. I know it will do the same for you. It has to, for as we will explore next, it is a law of the supernatural.

PART ONE

THE **POWER** OF **GOD'S SPOKEN** WORD

1

THE POWER OF ONE SPOKEN SENTENCE

The voice of God is the most powerful force in nature,
indeed the only force in nature, for all energy is here
only because the power-filled Word is being spoken.

—A. W. TOZER[1]

"WHEN I LOOK at your heavens," David expressed to the Lord, "the work of your fingers, the moon and the stars that you have established; what are human beings that you are mindful of them, mortals that you care for them?" (Ps. 8:3–4). David's words reflect his awe of God's creation and the perspective we all should keep. We would do well to make it a practice to look beyond our cityscapes with their skyscrapers, our celebrities and their fame, and our fashions and possessions—the works of human hands—and stand, as David did, in wonder of what God has made.

I intimately understand David's sentiments. Exploring and musing at God's creation is a passion of mine too. I love to take in the vistas of the natural wonders. Perhaps there are few things more breathtaking to me than the majesty of the mountains, the vastness of the ocean, the colors in a summer sunset, or the serenity found in a fresh blanket of new-fallen snow. What can equal gazing up on a clear night and getting lost in a sea of countless stars?

David's words are profound in noting that humanity and all its devices are futile in comparison. Certainly God's theater puts on a daily show infinitely greater than anything we could ever produce.

However, David minimized God's power, even unintentionally, by his words. He inaccurately described the grandeur of creation as "the work of [God's] fingers." To understand my daring accusation, we must go back to the beginning to read the biblical account of how the heavens, the earth, and all that is in them began.

> In the beginning when God created the heavens and the earth, the earth was a formless void and darkness covered the face of the deep.
>
> —Genesis 1:1–2

Here the Bible depicts the earth before creation as a "formless void." Don't allow the meaning of this to get lost in translation as some do. A "formless void" doesn't compare the creation to a piece of clay yet to be molded by a potter's hands. No, the original language gives a sneak peek into something much more fascinating and even more miraculous. The Hebrew words here are *tōhû* and *bōhû*, which can be translated as "nothing" and "empty." [2] To put it plainly, before creation the earth was nothing with nothing in it!

The implications of this are tremendous. Unlike you and me, who can create things only by using preexisting tools and materials, God had nothing to work with. Notice that the creation story doesn't recount that God devised a set of blueprints and went to work to build the cosmos. It doesn't report that He programmed lines of code or that He even lifted a finger at all. This is why David is mistaken in his description of the creation as the work of God's fingers. God didn't create with His hands; He created with His voice.

Here is how creation all began: "God *said*, 'Let there be light'; and there was light" (Gen. 1:3). That's it. The creation of everything was that simple yet that incomprehensible. Our human minds can't understand creation *ex nihilo*—that is, creation "out of nothing." And we certainly can't grasp the power of a spoken word creating anything. Yet this is the miracle of creation. God spoke and it was done instantaneously. The stars were hung. The planets were aligned. The earth was established. The boundaries of each were set. In total God made eight powerful declarations through which He immediately brought forth light, the sky, land, the sea, the sun, the moon, stars, living creatures, vegetation, and humankind.

The Power of God Embedded Within Creation

Words do no justice in depicting the might of our God who can create everything with only words. And I believe the author of Genesis tried to relate this awesome power to us by the name he chose to describe God—*Elohim*. In each of the eight declarations it was Elohim who spoke. There are many names given to God by those who encountered Him throughout the Old Testament. To be sure, each represents the same God but simply illustrates different attributes of who He is. These include *El Shaddai*, the "all-sufficient God"; *El Elyon*, the "most high God"; *Jehovah Rapha*, the "Lord that heals"; and *Jehovah Jireh*, the "Lord will provide," among others.[3]

The designation of *Elohim* to describe the one who spoke all creation into existence must be intentional. *Elohim* is the plural of *El*, which scholars trace to mean "strength," "might," or "power."[4] In other words, God's attributes of strength, power, and might are responsible for the conception of the cosmos.

As with any conception, the father's DNA is embedded in His creation. With His spoken Word His powerful, creative, and boundary-setting characteristics were planted deeply within the creation. These qualities are in the foundation of everything He fashioned. Perhaps this explains the power within natural resources to support and sustain life: how oxygen powers the cells of organisms, why water energizes our muscles, or how sunlight transfers energy. Perhaps this is how we harness their powers in our technology. Is this how gasoline converts into chemical and heat energy to fuel our vehicles? Or the molecules in the air provide for the travel of frequencies and radio waves of our cellular networks? I believe these natural resources, such as air, water, sunlight, plants, and oil, all work the way they do, even allowing us to tap into their power, because they contain the DNA of their almighty Creator.

The Dependable Laws of God

The universe is filled with constants. We call these phenomena laws. We take it for granted that these rules will be the same today as they were yesterday. These laws are the reasons behind many natural phenomena:[5]

- Gravity continues to hold objects down to earth.
- The speed of light remains constant at 186,000 miles per second.
- The earth rotates in twenty-four hours.
- Your hot coffee always cools off after sitting on the table for a while.

Adding astonishment to these facts is that these laws don't hold true only on earth. No, as American author and physicist James Trefil admits, these laws are in effect throughout the entire universe. He says, "The laws of nature we discover here and now in our laboratories are true everywhere in the universe and have been in force for all time."[6] How amazing! The laws of nature that we depend on here on earth are the same laws that govern the stars some billions of light-years away.[7]

Scientists are desperate to make sense of these laws and to uncover the origin of their behaviors, but their efforts to do so have only frustrated them. I recently stumbled across an online article titled "Scientists Baffled by Laws of Nature." Scientists say, "Doesn't it seem strange that our universe is so orderly?"[8] To the secularists who refuse to acknowledge any divine source, this is all reasoned away through a broad stroke of nature's evolutionary process.

But not all scientists are so cavalier to discount the consistency of creation to the equivalent of scientific fairy tales. Many see the miracle in it all—that the unchanging, dependable laws of nature reflect the qualities of a lawgiver. But not just any lawgiver, for these are the same qualities the Bible uses to describe God.

> For I the LORD do not change.
>
> —MALACHI 3:6

> Jesus Christ [God in the flesh] is the same yesterday and today and forever.
>
> —HEBREWS 13:8

The Bible asserts that God's qualities never change. His character, dependability, and power remain constant. We should not be surprised then that His creation reflects the same. This is the solution that dozens of famous historical scientists, such as Copernicus, Kepler, Galileo, Newton, and Pascal, proposed. In fact, their studies were all influenced by their faith. They believed that because God is steady and consistent, His universe must also be orderly and mathematically precise.[9] And as time and technology have proven—it is!

What Holds Everything Together?

Let's go a step further now. There is something even more fascinating than observing God's DNA in the laws of the universe. A mind-boggling scientific belief is that sound waves are at the very foundation of everything.

Without boring you with too much technical jargon, allow me to explain such a curious statement. Consider the basic science we all learned in high school—everything is made up of matter. I am made up of matter and you are made up of matter. Yes, everything that exists is made up of matter. Get the idea? This came from Einstein's proposal; remember $E = mc^2$? Basically Einstein suggests that matter consists of energy, which means that nothing in the universe is still. Instead, everything is actually vibrating to some degree. It is these vibrations that create sound waves.[10]

Others have since advanced Einstein's ideas in what is now referred to as superstring theory. I won't get into the details; I am not a scientist myself. But perhaps the simplest way to illustrate the concept is through something we all can imagine—a guitar. You tune a guitar by stretching the strings. Depending on the tension of the string and how it is plucked, the strings produce a variety of notes.[11] According to the theory, creation is held together by "a symphony of vibrating strings."[12] All matter is made up of vibrations, all at different tones and melodies.

Have I lost you? Fear not. The essence is this: scientists believe that everything in existence today—from the most microscopic elements to stars, planets, and galaxies—were all formed and continue to be sustained by sound waves.[13]

Did you get that? *Everything in creation was created by and continues to be held together by sound.*

The notion is staggering. Take a moment to look around from where you are right now. What do you see? This book? A chair, a couch, or a bed? A computer or a phone? A pet? A tree? Certainly your own body. Whatever you see, at the foundation of it—the glue that holds it together even now—is a sound. How unfathomably awesome!

One Spoken Sentence

Perhaps it seems as if we have cracked creation's code here, but this isn't a mystery only recently discovered by brilliant minds and modern technology. No, the truth behind creation has been right under our noses for some time now, boasted countless times per day throughout secular culture in our schools, in textbooks and magazines, and on television programs. The truth is found in the word we all use for the cosmos—*universe.*

Don't miss the spellbinding reality found in this word. *Universe* is derived from two Latin words: *unus*, which means "one," and *versus*, from which we get *verse*, which denotes a spoken sentence.[14]

Let's put this together now. Plainly defined, the universe is "one spoken sentence." Let that sink in! With this, we need not wonder how or what made the universe exist because the answer is found in the word itself. The universe is one spoken sentence. It came into being by one spoken sentence. And as we have seen so far, everything in it is upheld by one spoken sentence.

I even dare profess to know the exact sentence responsible for the creation and the One who spoke it. *Elohim*, our Creator, almighty God of infinite strength, power, and might, declared into the void, "Let there be...!" Instantly the power of who He is, activated by His spoken Word, went to work to create the heavens, the earth, and all that is in them.

Isn't this astonishing? I marvel how God seems to set up these things so that all throughout the world people are constantly proclaiming the truth that He created everything by the power of His spoken Word.

The Ultimate, Supernatural Law

As we have learned, sound is simply made up of vibrations. When a bell rings, a drum resounds, or someone speaks, the vibrations put out by the instrument cause the air around to vibrate, including the air inside your ears, creating sound.[15] We know that eventually the sound dissipates and can no longer be heard. This is great news in many cases! Still, while the noise diminishes, the sound waves are actually converted into energy. And this energy remains in existence—forever!

Though we no longer hear the actual voice of God declaring His creating words, the power from them still exists. Like an infinite echo the power of God's Word still reverberates throughout the cosmos. And now, so many years later, the power of His words still holds all things together.

Scientific discovery is slowly catching up to what is already recorded in Scripture! Notice how everything we have explored so far is described throughout the Bible.

- Everything was created by the power of God's Word.

  In the beginning was the Word, and the Word was with God, and the Word was God.

  —JOHN 1:1

  By faith we understand that the universe was created by the word of God, so that what is seen was not made out of things that are visible.

  —HEBREWS 11:3, ESV

  By the word of God heavens existed long ago and an earth was formed out of water and by means of water.

  —2 PETER 3:5

- Everything is upheld by the power of God's Word.

  He is the reflection of God's glory and the exact imprint of God's very being, and he sustains all things by his powerful word.

  —HEBREWS 1:3

It is evident that God's Word is the most powerful force in the universe. I like to think of its power as a supernatural law. Embedded into everything from the beginning, it is what established all the other so-called laws of nature. Therefore, it is certainly the most foundational. What else in nature can create from nothing? Nothing! Nature can only reproduce from something that already exists. Nothing else holds together and sustains all things. Nothing is as dependable. Not gravity. Not the tides. Not even the speed of light. The attributes displayed by God's spoken Word are all nothing short of supernatural. Nothing else can accomplish what the Word does.

"Let There Be..." in You!

God spoke and His will was done. That is limitless power. As A. W. Tozer profoundly said, "In the beginning He spoke to nothing, and it became *something*. Chaos heard it and became order, darkness heard it and became light."[16] I envision God's spoken Word as a container of strength, power, and might. The Bible assures that the release of His Word from His mouth is the activation of a force that goes to work to do whatever He sets it out to do.

> So shall my word be that goes out from my mouth; it shall not return to me empty, but it shall accomplish that which I purpose, and succeed in the thing for which I sent it.
>
> —ISAIAH 55:11

There are no ifs, ands, or buts about it—God's Word works! Let's summarize its powerful work in what we observe through the creation story.

The Word	The Work
"In the beginning...the earth was a formless void..." (Gen. 1:1–2).	God's spoken Word gave *identity* to what was meaningless.
"...while a wind from God swept over the face of the waters" (Gen. 1:2).	God's spoken Word brought *peace* and calm to what was chaotic.
"In the beginning...darkness covered the face of the deep.... Then God said, 'Let there be light'; and there was light" (Gen. 1:1–3).	God's spoken Word brought *light* into that which was dark.
"And God separated the light from the darkness. God called the light Day, and the darkness he called Night" (Gen. 1:4–5).	God's spoken Word gave *structure* to that which had none.
"And God said, 'Let there be a dome in the midst of the waters, and let it separate the waters from the waters'" (Gen. 1:6).	God's spoken Word set *boundaries* that could never be crossed.
"And God said, 'Let the waters bring forth swarms of living creatures'" (Gen. 1:20).	God's spoken Word brought *life* out of things that were lifeless.

The Word	The Work
"Then God said, 'Let us make humankind in our image, according to our likeness; and let them have dominion...over every creeping thing that creeps upon the earth'" (Gen. 1:26).	God's spoken Word gave *authority* and power to humankind.

God's spoken words at creation established tangibles such as the stars, planets, dirt, animals, and people. And it continues to hold all these together. But as we learned from the chart above, it also created things that may be harder to see but are just as important: attributes such as identity, peace, light, structure, boundaries, life, and authority.

We have just explored the limitless power of God's spoken Word at creation. But now consider that God has spoken many more words, all of which are equally as powerful. We need not search high and low for these words as if they are lost and need to be found. No, He has given us countless more, all inspired (spoken from His mouth) and placed in plain sight within our Bibles. These words, put into sixty-six books, are collectively known as the Word of God.

This is great news for you and me! God gave His Word not only to power creation, but to power our lives too. As you will discover as you continue reading, God's spoken Word establishes the identity, peace, light, structure, boundaries, life, and authority of creation in your life and circumstances. But it also does so much more. Because of His spoken Word you don't have to feel purposeless any longer. Stress will fade away as you apply His refreshment to your soul. Obstacles will no longer be a hindrance when you stand on the reality of His promises. Battles will be won once you learn to live in His victory. These are the awesome benefits of living inside the power of "one spoken sentence."

Today God declares, "Let there be..." in you!

2

THE BIBLICAL PRINCIPLE OF SPEAKING SCRIPTURE

WHEN I QUOTE SCRIPTURE, I KNOW I AM QUOTING THE VERY WORD OF GOD. —BILLY GRAHAM[1]

THE EXPRESSION "My word is my bond" was coined many years ago. Some trace its origins back to the 1500s Scottish proverb "An Englishman's word is his bond."[2] This was said at a time when an agreement was made by the mere integrity of a good man's spoken acknowledgment, back when an "I will do it" was enough to bind a contract.

Others contend that the concept dates back much farther, to the first few verses of Scripture. As we explored in chapter 1, when God declared, "Let there be light," there was light. Thus it is said that "My word is my bond" was influenced by the core belief that whenever God gives His Word, it is done.

God's spoken Word cannot be separated from who He is: *El Hanne'eman*, the faithful God who maintains His covenants (Deut. 7:9). In fact, because God's people knew Him as nothing but loyal, they never had a Hebrew word for *promise*. That is, there was never a distinction between something God said and something He guaranteed. People always assumed that whatever God spoke would happen. Let me explain.

The first time *promise* is used in our English Bibles (see NRSV) is during the account of God's spoken word to Abraham and Sarah regarding the birth of their son, Isaac. Multiple times God

11

assured the couple that they would have a child despite their old age and Sarah's apparent barrenness. In Genesis 21:1 the author recorded that God made good on His Word: "The LORD dealt with Sarah as he had said, and the LORD did for Sarah as he had *promised.*" The original word here for "promise" is a not a Hebrew equivalent, but *dābar*, which simply means "to say." [3] This is true throughout the remainder of the Old Testament. In each case, the Hebrew word for "promise" is either a form of *'āmar* or *dābar*, both of which mean someone said or spoke. It wasn't until many years later that English translators chose to use *promise* when the word was found within a future context. [4]

What we have learned here is possibly one of the most foundational principles of Scripture: when God speaks, He promises. There are no caveats, no qualifying statements, and no asterisks to denote a disclaimer. For some this may seem obvious. We know, at least theologically, that God does not and cannot lie. So you might think, "Yes, of course His Word is a promise." But for many others it is comforting and reassuring to know that God's Word is not the same as that of a human, susceptible to failure or fraud. No, God's Word is sure to happen. His Word is a signature inked in heaven that cannot be annulled but is supernaturally binding and everlasting.

Balaam's second oracle in the Book of Numbers illustrates this point well. God prophesies through Balaam:

> God is not a human being, that he should lie, or a mortal, that he should change his mind. Has he *promised*, and will he not do it? Has he spoken, and will he not fulfill it?
>
> —NUMBERS 23:19

In the original language, Balaam asserts, "Has he *said*, and will he not do it? Has he spoken, and will he not fulfill it?" Of course these are meant as rhetorical questions. As we learned, God's spoken Word is a force that accomplishes whatever it sets out to do (Isa. 55:11). In other words, God's Word is His bond.

The Authority of God's Word

We all know that the weight of what is spoken and the likelihood of it happening often depend on who said it. If someone broke into my house to steal my belongings, I would understandably be upset and have some things to say to the thief. Still, my words could only wound his emotions; they could not impose a penalty. The words of a judge, however, can do some real damage.

The difference between the power of my words and those of a judge has nothing to do with superficial characteristics such as physical stature, age, or location of birth. Rather, it is the judge's designated *authority*, backed by character and integrity, that gives her or his words influence.

Teaching at length about the authority of God would be pointless, for why and how He has authority should be blatantly obvious. He is, after all, the Creator of the heavens, the earth, and all that is in them (Ps. 146:6). Almighty, Most High, King of kings, and Lord of lords are just a number of the names used to describe His supremacy.

When God speaks, His Words contain the authority of His majesty, which all creation obeys. This is why mountains quake and hills bow down at the mention of His name. His Words are also backed by His character: holy, just, truthful, merciful, loving, faithful, and dependable, just to name a few of His tremendous attributes.

This is precisely what David celebrated in the Psalms. "I give you thanks, O LORD, with my whole heart," he expressed. "[I] give thanks to your name for your steadfast love and your faithfulness; for you have exalted your name and your word above everything" (Ps. 138:1–2). In essence, David explained that God's Word is empowered by and carries the authority of His name and His character. This is why His Word is equal to His name. This is what makes it so powerful.

The Delegation of God's Word

Up until now I have taught the obvious: God's Word, spoken directly out of His mouth, is powerful to accomplish whatever He intends for it to accomplish. But within the very definition of the word *authority* is a bit less apparent truth, yet one that the Scriptures most certainly teach.

> Authority: the right to act in a specified way, delegated from one person or organization to another[5]

The key word in this definition is *delegated*, which involves two functions: the power to enact someone else's word and/or the power to speak with someone else's authority. Let's explore what Scripture has to say about each of these functions in relation to God's Word.

The power to enact God's Word

To continue my earlier judicial illustration, the judge does not leave the bench to implement the sentence after a ruling but instead assigns people—bailiffs, officers, counselors, and others—to carry out his or her words. This is part of delegated authority.

God too has empowered others with the role of ensuring that His Word is enacted. In fact, this is one of the primary tasks of the angels.

> Bless the LORD, O you his angels, you mighty ones who *do his word*, obeying the voice of his word!
>
> —PSALM 103:20, ESV

What this psalm reveals is that God has delegated authority to the angels to enact His Word. Think about the voice activation of your modern smartphone assistant. When you speak, "Hey, Siri!" or "OK, Google!" the phone comes to life and awaits your command. I certainly don't intend to portray the angels as robots, but I imagine that they are "always on," listening for God's Word. And when they hear it, they go to work to help make it happen.

The power to speak God's Word

The psalm above uncovers a fascinating concept that you have possibly never considered. It describes the role of the angels as "obeying the *voice* of [God's] word" (Ps. 103:20, ESV). But what does this mean? We know the Bible is considered the Word of God. So does the psalm intend to say that the angels scour Scripture to make God's words happen? Perhaps. But I believe the word *voice* is crucial to understand the full meaning. One author illustrates it in this way: "Take your Bible and place it next to your ear. Stop! Listen! What do you hear? Nothing! Why? Because the Bible does not have a voice unless *we* give it a voice."[6]

We—Christians—are given God's Word to speak. Speaking it is how we give it a voice. In essence, this is what Paul wrote about in his detailing of the full armor of God. He said that in Christ we are clothed in God's power and given a belt for truth, a breastplate for righteousness, shoes for peace, a shield for faith, a helmet for salvation, and a sword, which is the Word of God (Eph. 6:10–17). Indeed, Christians have been given these pieces of armor as gifts from God to use for our benefit. This is delegated authority.

You and I are able to give voice to God's Word so that when we speak it, it maintains God's authority as if He has spoken it Himself. When you speak a declaration of the Scripture in Philippians 4:6, "I am not anxious for anything," you give voice to God's Word, activating the angels to bring peace that surpasses all understanding (Phil. 4:7). When you declare 1 Corinthians 10:13, saying, "No temptation will overtake me," the angels respond to it by providing a way of escape.

The Transfer of Life

Only something that is living can create and reproduce. When God declared, "Let there be..." into the void at creation, these words were pregnant with His life, which gave them their creating power. And as we have seen, the life that flowed from God's words still runs through the veins of creation today, sustaining and upholding everything.

All throughout its pages the Bible confirms the truth of the life in God's words. Speaking to the children of Israel about what sustained them in the wilderness, Moses assured that it wasn't the manna God provided, but that the sustenance of their lives is "every word that comes from the mouth of the LORD" (Deut. 8:3). Famished from fasting for forty days, Jesus reaffirmed the truth of the life and nourishment of God's Word during His temptation by reciting to the devil Moses's words (Matt. 4:4). Teaching His disciples about the very source of life, Jesus left no room for doubt. "The words that I have spoken to you are spirit and life," He instructed (John 6:63). Paul encouraged young Timothy to remain close to the Scripture, which is beaming with life. "All scripture is inspired [given life] by God," he wrote (2 Tim. 3:16). To the Hebrews, Paul reiterated a similar point: "Indeed, the word of God is living and active" (Heb. 4:12).

That God's Word still contains life is a key to understanding its miracle-working and transformational power today. To put it simply, God's Word gives life to whatever it is applied to because it is the very source of life itself.

Proverbs famously teaches that our tongues also have the power to give this life:

> Death and life are in the power of the tongue, and those
> who love it will eat its fruits.
> —PROVERBS 18:21

Obviously this verse does not mean that we can lick things to life with our tongues! As it is often used throughout the Bible, the word *tongue* here is used to mean words. We all know the power of our words either to wound or to build up. Many relationships have been destroyed simply because of the power of death that can come from idle or negative words. We also know the encouragement and confidence that can be given through a single positive affirmation.

Of course nothing is more powerful for transformation, encouragement, faith building, or the activation of miracles than speaking the ultimate source of life—the Word of God itself. And throughout the Bible this is precisely how God instructed His Word to be used. Let's explore some of these examples now.

Success from speaking the Word

After wandering in the wilderness for forty years, the time had come for the children of Israel to finally possess the land God promised. But now that their original leader, Moses, had passed away, the next up, Joshua, needed confidence to take over. In His commission, here's what the Lord told Joshua would be the secret sauce to his success:

> This book of the law shall not depart out of your mouth;
> you shall meditate on it day and night, so that you may be
> careful to act in accordance with all that is written in it. For
> then you shall make your way prosperous, and then you
> shall be successful.
>
> —JOSHUA 1:8

Throughout the Old Testament, the *book of the law* is synonymous with God's Word. That is simply what they knew it as. Here God made clear to Joshua that prosperity and success are dependent on a practice of keeping God's Word in His mouth or in other words, a habit of speaking it.

The Word as the source of refreshment

In most books an introduction prepares readers for what is ahead and instructs them in how to use the book. The first chapter of Psalms serves as the book's introduction, and the first few verses prepare us well for how to use the words that come after.

> Happy are those who do not follow the advice of the wicked,
> or take the path that sinners tread, or sit in the seat of

scoffers; but their delight is in the law of the LORD, and on
his law they meditate day and night.

—PSALM 1:1–2

Again, *law* is used to mean God's Word, on which the psalmist
instructed people to "meditate day and night." Those of us in contemporary Christianity might not immediately recognize what is
meant here by meditating on God's Word, or perhaps we mistake it for modern meditation, which is often nothing more than
intently thinking about something. The Jewish practice of meditation, however, didn't only consist of thinking and memorizing;
it involved a very emotional process of speaking. In fact, part of
the Hebrew definition of *meditate* (Heb. *hagah*) is "to speak."[7]

Happiness is promised to those who find delight in God's Word
and who speak it day and night. "They are like trees planted by
streams of water, which yield their fruit in its season, and their
leaves do not wither," the psalm continues. "In all that they do,
they prosper" (Ps. 1:3). This is a beautiful illustration of refreshment. Whereas you and I might think of trees in a lush forest, the
original reader knew mostly of trees in the midst of a desert. This
makes the illustration all the more powerful. Those who speak
God's Word on a regular basis will experience the refreshment that
streams provide sun-scorched trees that are desperate for water.

Restoration from speaking the Word

Over time the disobedience of God's people left the nation of
Israel defiled by their enemies, scattered, and in ruins. But God
often used prophets to foretell of their restoration. Ezekiel was
one of these prophets.

The Lord came to Ezekiel in a vision, placing him amid a valley
of countless dry bones. Ezekiel understood this to be representa-
tive of the state of God's people—lifeless and scattered. Then God
instructed Ezekiel to prophesy—to speak—His Word to the bones.

O dry bones, hear the word of the LORD. Thus says the
Lord GOD to these bones: I will cause breath to enter you,

and you shall live. I will lay sinews on you, and will cause flesh to come upon you, and cover you with skin, and put breath in you, and you shall live; and you shall know that I am the LORD.

—EZEKIEL 37:4–6

Ezekiel reported that as he spoke God's Word to these bones, he immediately began to see the bones come back together, covered with skin and empowered with life. Certainly the Lord could have restored the nation of Israel back to life without any of this, yet He used His Word, spoken through a human, to initiate the restoration.

The activation of miracles from speaking the Word

The New Testament provides numerous examples of the spoken Word to transfer death or life. Jesus's words to a fig tree, for example, caused it to wither up and die. "May no one ever eat fruit from you again," He matter-of-factly cursed (Mark 11:14).

You might be thinking, "Well, yes, Jesus's words are understandably powerful; He is God!" But we must remember that while on earth, Jesus emptied Himself of His Godhood and took on the form of a human (Phil. 2:7). He performed all His miracles and endured His crucifixion, not because He was God, but because He was empowered with the Holy Spirit. Our hope of doing the same and greater things than Jesus did depends on this being true (John 14:12). We will never be God, but we do have access to the same Spirit who empowered Jesus (Rom. 8:11).

Furthermore, just a few verses later, Jesus revealed to His disciples that they too could do what He did:

> Truly I tell you, if you say to this mountain, "Be taken up and thrown into the sea," and if you do not doubt in your heart, but believe that what you say will come to pass, it will be done for you.

—MARK 11:23

In other words, Jesus instructed His disciples that they could speak to any situation, circumstance, or obstacle and tell it to go. He assured that their words, coupled with faith, would bring it to pass.

The disciples obviously took Jesus's teachings to heart; they routinely employed the practice of speaking to activate miracles. In the Book of Acts alone, *all* the miracles detailed by Peter and Paul were accompanied by a declaration founded in the truth of God's Word.

Miracle	Declaration
Peter heals a lame man (Acts 3:1–11).	"In the name of Jesus Christ of Nazareth, stand up and walk" (Acts 3:6).
Peter heals a paralyzed man (Acts 9:33–34).	"Aeneas, Jesus Christ heals you; get up and make your bed!" (Acts 9:34).
Peter raises a woman from the dead (Acts 9:36–41).	"Tabitha, get up" (Acts 9:40).
Peter heals a crippled man (Acts 14:8–10).	"Stand upright on your feet" (Acts 14:10).
Paul casts out an evil spirit (Acts 16:16–18).	"I order you in the name of Jesus Christ to come out of her" (Acts 16:18).
Paul restores a man to life (Acts 20:9–12).	"Do not be alarmed, for his life is in him" (Acts 20:10).
Paul heals a man of fever and dysentery (Acts 28:8).	No quote is given. But the verse indicates that the man was healed by a spoken prayer and laying on of hands.

More than all these, however, the greatest miracle and transfer of life is the gift of salvation, which gives eternal life. Even this miracle is activated by a spoken word:

> If you confess with your lips that Jesus is Lord and believe
> in your heart that God raised him from the dead, you will
> be saved.
>
> —ROMANS 10:9

As we see in these examples, speaking the Word of God acti-
vates its power to bring success and prosperity, refreshment, and
restoration; to overcome obstacles; and to perform miracles.

I have gone into great detail with all this to build your confidence in the biblical principle that God delegates the power and
authority of His Word to His people. Whether spoken directly
from His mouth or spoken through you and me, God's Word
is His bond. It never falters; it never fails. It will uphold you
through anything you currently face and whatever the future
brings. Angels are ready and waiting to ensure that it happens!

3

HOW TO PUT THE WORD TO WORK FOR YOU

I like in my time of trouble to find a promise which exactly fits my need, and then to put my finger on it, and say, "Lord, this is thy word; I beseech thee to prove that it is so, by carrying it out in my case."

—CHARLES SPURGEON[1]

As a child, Linda was plagued with panic attacks, tormenting thoughts, and what-ifs that paralyzed her with fear. "When I grew older, I could literally feel anxiety attack my mind and body," she recalls.

As these evil darts continued to bombard her mind, Linda searched for relief. But unfortunately, her search led her only into further darkness. "Over time I slipped further and further from the presence of God," she admits. "I began to reach out for help using the things of the world. Drinking and partying became my escape. But this only led to more guilt, shame, and anxiety."

For fourteen years Linda was bound to this cycle of defeat. And just as soon as she'd experience a bit of victory, the attacks would begin again. "My mind was so filled with fear and torment that I thought I would end up in an institution. I would hear whispers such as, 'You are not worthy of God's healing.'" The tormenting thoughts occurred anywhere and anytime, and eventually entered her dreams until she could no longer sleep at night. "Everywhere I went, anxiety engulfed me," she said.

Thankfully Linda's story didn't end in despair. At possibly her lowest point, God placed an anointed woman in her life—one who could relate from undergoing similar spiritual attacks on her own life. The woman began to mentor her and teach her about the promises that God's Word contains for any situation. "She showed me something I had never heard before," Linda explained. "She taught me how to overcome the lies being shot into my mind by speaking God's Word." She began with 2 Timothy 1:7: "For God gave us a spirit not of fear but of power and love and self-control" (ESV). "I stood on that scripture with everything in me," Linda shared. "Every time I started to feel anxious, I spoke it aloud."

Feeling the results of this newfound practice, Linda turned to the Bible for more of God's promises. When she would find a promise that related to a struggle, she would write it down and begin to speak the promise aloud—daily—until she experienced victory. "I used these scriptures as spiritual weapons," she exclaimed. "Every day I became a little stronger, and one day I realized I was no longer being attacked."

Certainly Linda is an avid believer in the power of God's Word. And she understandably talks about it as much as she can. By activating the Word's power through speaking the Word aloud on a regular basis, she allowed it to completely transform her life. It gave her peace to overcome anxiety, hope instead of despair, and freedom from the bondage of addiction.[2]

The Source of Strongholds

Linda's early years illustrate the usual schemes in the devil's playbook:

- Bombarding the mind with lies, doubts, and what-ifs
- Presenting an object (money, fame, career), a substance (drugs, alcohol), or a person (an unhealthy, codependent relationship) as the means of relief

- When the person succumbs to the pressures, following up by giving intense guilt and shame

Linda experienced the extreme difficulty of getting off this merry-go-round. Often the guilt and shame are also accompanied with more lies, doubts, and what-ifs. "Look what you've done!" the enemy will taunt. "You're too far gone." As hopelessness and despair are added to the original stressors, the person continues to search for ways of relief, likely returning to familiar crutches. And around and around it goes.

This vicious cycle is the enemy's most poignant form of attack, known as a stronghold. Instructing the Corinthian church about the obstacles they will face, Paul warns them of such attacks:

> Indeed, we live as human beings, but we do not wage war according to human standards; for the weapons of our warfare are not merely human, but they have divine power to destroy strongholds.
> —2 CORINTHIANS 10:3–4

Paul defines *strongholds* as supernatural vises that just won't let go. He continues to describe them as "arguments" (2 Cor. 10:5, ESV) and proud obstacles "raised up against the knowledge of God" (2 Cor. 10:5, NASB).

The word here for *arguments* is the Greek word *logismos*, which means "reasoning."[3] This obviously involves the mind, which is precisely how the enemy enters to build a stronghold. He wants your mind to "reason away" the knowledge of God, or in other words, to doubt the truth of God's Word. Through reasoning Satan seeks to erode your confidence that God's Word is certain to happen in your life.

Here are some common arguments he uses against the truth of God's Word. Perhaps you will recognize some of them at work in your own life.

God's Word	Satan's Counterargument
"So in Christ Jesus you are all children of God through faith" (Gal. 3:26, NIV).	Nobody has ever really wanted you; you are just an accident.
"Anyone who belongs to Christ has become a new person. The old life is gone; a new life has begun!" (2 Cor. 5:17, NLT).	You will always struggle with the same old struggles; you will never be free.
"God made Him who knew no sin to be sin for us, that we might become the righteousness of God in Him" (2 Cor. 5:21, MEV).	You are just a poor, pathetic sinner; you can't do anything right. God will never forgive you.
"Neither death nor life, neither angels nor principalities nor powers, neither things present nor things to come, neither height nor depth, nor any other created thing, shall be able to separate us from the love of God, which is in Christ Jesus our Lord" (Rom. 8:38–39, MEV).	Look at the things you've done. Nobody's ever really loved you; nobody will ever love you. God doesn't love you either.
"For in Christ lives all the fullness of God in a human body. So you also are complete through your union with Christ" (Col. 2:9–10, NLT).	You are not married! You are not educated enough; you haven't achieved enough! You are just not good enough!
"For we are God's masterpiece. He has created us anew in Christ Jesus, so we can do the good things he planned for us long ago" (Eph. 2:10, NLT)	You have no purpose. God has forgotten about you. Your life is hopeless.

In each of these examples Satan's argument is obviously completely counter to the truth of God's Word; nevertheless, we often fail to see the obvious in our own lives. This is because each one of the devil's arguments is accompanied with evidence from the past. He will use your father's betrayal of your family to convince you that you are merely an accident. He will use your mistake last week as reason to believe you will always continue to struggle. He will use a failed relationship as evidence to support the idea that nobody will ever love you. And so on.

Paul instructed that these arguments are "proud obstacles," meaning that they are set up to trip you up—over and over again (2 Cor. 10:4–5, NLT). The lie that starts in the mind is then soon lived out through habitual, defeated behavior.

Divine Dynamite

Thankfully God doesn't leave people to be the devil's doormat. No, He gives us weapons of warfare to destroy any strongholds that would hold us back or hold us down.

First, know that the ability to destroy strongholds does not come from our own flesh. Positive thinking, self-help, an exercise plan, a good diet—none of these are strong enough to break the enemy's holds. Only something with divine power can release the grip of something with a supernatural hold.

It may be difficult to comprehend the magnitude of this "divine power" (2 Cor. 10:5). But the original language exposes something I believe we all can grasp. The word *power* here is *dynatos* in the Greek. This is the word from which we get our English word *dynamite*. Do you get the picture? God has given us supernatural, divine dynamite, not merely to weaken the strongholds of the enemy, but to completely blow up and obliterate them!

What specifically are these weapons, and how do we use them? In his letter to the Ephesians, Paul wrote from a Roman prison, illustrating some of these supernatural gifts as pieces of the uniform in which the guards around him were outfitted. "Be strong in the Lord and in the strength of his power," Paul instructed. "Put on the whole armor of God, so that you may be able to stand against the wiles of the devil" (Eph. 6:10–11). He continued on to describe the enemy, asserting, "Our struggle is against our coworkers, in-laws, spouse, children, and political foes." I am only joking. No, Paul was consistent with what he maintained throughout all his letters: people are not our enemies—the devil is.

> For our struggle is not against enemies of blood and flesh,
> but against the rulers, against the authorities, against the

cosmic powers of this present darkness, against the spiritual forces of evil in the heavenly places.

—EPHESIANS 6:12

Paul then went on to detail the weapons God gives us for victory over these spiritual forces of evil. This "whole armor of God" consists of a belt of truth, a breastplate of righteousness, shoes of peace, a shield of faith, a helmet of salvation, and a sword, which is God's Word. (See Ephesians 6:14–17.)

In my book *Silence Satan*, I explain each of these articles with a fascinating look into their historical and modern applications.[4] I won't take the time to recount it all here. I do, however, want to draw your attention to what I mentioned in the introduction of this book. Open your Bible and reread Ephesians 6:10–17, the passage about the whole armor of God. Note the word *stand* throughout. Here are the highlights:

Put on the whole armor of God, so that you may be able to *stand* against the wiles of the devil.

—VERSE 11

Therefore take up the whole armor of God, so that you may be able to *withstand* on that evil day, and having done everything, to *stand* firm.

—VERSE 13

Stand therefore, and fasten the belt of truth around your waist, and put on the breastplate of righteousness.

—VERSE 14

Notice that Paul didn't instruct to put on the whole armor of God so that you may be able to *fight* against the devil. No, he chose to use the word *stand* four times throughout the passage to describe how we are to use each piece as a spiritual weapon— not to fight a devil who is defeated, but to *stand* in the victory of Jesus, the One who defeated him.

In the chart below, I have paralleled each piece in the whole armor of God to a different aspect of who Christ is.

Piece of Armor	Who Christ Is
Belt of *truth*	"I am the way, and the *truth*, and the life" (John 14:6).
Breastplate of *righteousness*	"He is the source of your life in Christ Jesus, who became for us wisdom from God, and *righteousness* and sanctification and redemption" (1 Cor. 1:30).
Shoes of *peace*	"I have said this to you, so that in me you may have *peace*" (John 16:33).
Shield of *faith*	"Looking to Jesus the pioneer and perfecter of our *faith*" (Heb. 12:2).
Helmet of *salvation*	"There is *salvation* in no one else, for there is no other name under heaven given among mortals by which we must be saved" (Acts 4:12).
Sword of the Spirit (the *Word* of God)	"And the *Word* became flesh and lived among us" (John 1:14).

Paul essentially revealed that those who are "in Christ" (Christians) are already protected by the pieces of this supernatural uniform. Jesus is truth. He is the source of righteousness. Our peace is in Him. He is the foundation of our faith. He provides our salvation. He is the living expression of God's Word. To put it simply, Jesus is our armor. His weapons are "weapons of righteousness" (2 Cor. 6:7). They are rays of light that penetrate any darkness. This divine dynamite is the power of His might, which obliterated the works of the enemy at the cross once and for all (Col. 2:14–15). It is now given to us as a force field of victory to live in and stand on.

Wielding Your Weapon

The final piece in the armor—the sword of the Spirit—provides the key to activating the first five weapons. It is what we use to stand firm in Christ's victory against the lies of the enemy.

Paul equated the Roman soldier's sword to God's Word. From a historical perspective the sword was the only piece of the armor that had an offensive function. That is, it was often waved in the air by the soldier as a threat to oncoming enemies. In this function the soldier didn't need to leave his position to engage the enemy. No, he could simply stand in the protection of the rest of his armor by wielding his sword to declare, "I'm armed and dangerous—stay back!"

Perhaps by now you are getting the revelation of how this compares to how we are to put God's Word to work in our lives. But the original language uncovers more insight into how Paul meant for this sword to be used.

As we just reviewed, Jesus is the Word of God in the flesh. John's Gospel couldn't be any clearer: "In the beginning was the Word, and the Word was with God, and the Word was God" (John 1:1). John continued, saying that in Jesus "the Word became flesh and lived among us" (John 1:14). At this point people often ask, "How can Jesus and the Bible both be the Word of God?" This is a reasonable question because obviously Jesus is a person and the Bible is a book.

In John's Gospel the Greek word for *Word* is *logos*. And *logos* is used all throughout the New Testament to describe the message of God. Scripture is the written message of God. But here John revealed Jesus as the embodiment of God's written message.[5] He is the One of whom the prophets foretold. He is the fulfillment of all God's promises. He is the very reason we know that God's word is His bond. Through Jesus, God did and continues to do everything He promised.

In writing about the whole armor, Paul chose to use a different word for *Word*. He chose the Greek word *rhema*. While *rhema* is also translated as "word" all throughout the English New Testament, there is a nuanced difference. Whereas *logos* generally refers to the *essence* of God's Word, *rhema* indicates God's Word when it is spoken.[6] We see this, for example, when Jesus quoted Moses: "One does not live by bread alone, but by every word [*rhema*] that comes from the mouth of God" (Matt. 4:4).

As one highly educated in Jewish tradition, the apostle Paul understood the principle of keeping God's Word running through your mouth. He knew that speaking God's Word is the activation of its power to give life and success, to overcome obstacles, and to perform miracles—the very things we explored in the previous chapter. And now he instructed that the spoken Word of God, *rhema*, is a sword given to us by God to sever the strongholds of the enemy and to stand on everything we have in Christ.

Ways to Speak the Word

The obvious way to use a sword is to take it out of its sheath. And how we put God's Word to work in this way is to give voice to it—to speak it. Just as Linda declared God's Word as the cure for anxiety, we too can stand on its promises and activate its power to tear down strongholds, win spiritual battles, and ultimately transform our lives. The Bible teaches at least three ways to give voice to God's Word.

Declarations

Numerous ministers have attempted to count the number of promises made directly to God's people in Scripture. I have heard estimates ranging between three thousand and seven thousand. I haven't taken the time to count them myself, but suffice it to say, there are many. These promises give tremendous assurances about what we should count on and stand on regardless of how discouraging our circumstances seem.

When God spoke the promise of descendants to Abraham, he

and his wife were in what any realist would proclaim was an impossible situation for this to come to pass. Yet it was into this impossibility that God declared, "I will make of you a great nation...and in you all the families of the earth shall be blessed" (Gen. 12:2–3).

I am not sure I can think of any personal promise more substantial than to be the conduit of blessing for "all the families of the earth." Possibly more amazing though is that God includes you and me in Abraham's promise. "If you belong to Christ," Paul said, "then you are Abraham's offspring, heirs according to the promise" (Gal. 3:29). Yes, the promises of blessings given to Abraham are also promises to you and me!

The way to stand on a promise is to announce it over your life or your situation. This is called a *declaration*. In this case you may declare, "Because I share in the inheritance of Abraham, I declare that I am blessed to be a blessing." Since the promise also includes your offspring, you should speak it over your children too: "I declare that my children are blessed so much that they too can meet the needs of others."

Additionally, declaring biblical promises about your health is a great way to put the power of God's Word to work for your everyday life. You should certainly do this when you are struggling with a symptom or an issue, but why not do so even when you are enjoying good health as a preventative measure? Scripture assures that "by [Jesus's] stripes we are healed" (Isa. 53:5, MEV). Extend your faith with the truth of this promise and declare it: "Because the wounds of Christ provided my healing, sickness has no place in me. I declare that I am healed in Jesus's name!" In the next four parts, we will engage with many more promises the Bible gives for life-changing results.

Finally, declarations are not simply statements you forcefully speak according to your own selfish will. You can't declare to have a mansion in Malibu and then expect God to do your bidding. No, declarations are about aligning your faith with God's will, which is found in His Word. Prayerfully search the Scripture for what God says related to your future, your health, or the difficulties you face, and then declare it. By earnestly announcing the promise, you stand with the truth of God's Word, activating angels to bring it to pass.

Commands

In chapter 2 we reviewed Jesus's promise that we may tell a mountain to move and it will move (Mark 11:23). This is what is known as a *command*.

We know that Jesus often used figures of speech to add emphasis to His teachings. His instructions for moving mountains are no different. Here, Jesus wasn't assuring that we can stand in front of Mount Everest and actually get it to move. No, He used *mountain* as a metaphor for a seemingly impossible situation. And that is actually great news for us. While we'd rarely (if ever) have the need to move an actual mountain, we often face situations that feel as gigantic as Mount Everest. Thankfully, regardless of how big or how small the problem, Jesus offers us the authority to command these obstacles to go.

Struggling with a bad attitude? Couple your command with a promise from Scripture: "The joy of the Lord is my strength. I command this bad attitude to go in Jesus's name." (See Nehemiah 8:10.) Feeling held back by fear? Declare this: "I do not have a spirit of fear, but of power, love, and a sound mind. Fear must get out of here!" (See 2 Timothy 1:7.) Suffering with a headache? Commanding it to "go in Jesus's name" might be all you need to do to experience relief.

Lastly, I want to draw your attention to what Jesus pronounced as essential for any command (or any spoken scripture) to be effective. After assuring that we have the ability to move mountains with our words, He instructs: "If you do not doubt in your heart, but believe that what you say will come to pass, it will be done for you" (Mark 11:23). Yes, the spoken Word must always be accompanied by faith.

I believe that God requires pairing the spoken Word with faith so that we don't turn this practice into something robotic. An unbeliever, for example, can't meaninglessly recite a scripture and see it come to pass. No, the results of speaking God's Word require the faith of a believer, the positive expectation of a Christian who is absolutely convinced that God's Word will happen.

Confessions

Growing up in a liturgical tradition, I regularly recited with other worshippers the "Profession of Faith" as a way to acknowledge my beliefs. "I believe in one God, the Father Almighty, Maker of heaven and earth…," our congregation would speak in unison.

In a similar way we can individually acknowledge the truths of Scripture to assure ourselves of who God says we are and what He says we have. This is a *confession*. The chart at the beginning of this chapter gave a handful of these promises. God's Word asserts that you are chosen, accepted, and made worthy, for example. As Linda discovered, God's Word promises that you are free from fear, anxiety, and so much more.

Scripture confessions are one of my favorite ways to put the Word to work in my life. A confession has the power to give an instant boost to battle whatever you face. But as we will explore, when spoken regularly, confessions are especially effective over time to change your thinking, which then changes your behavior, which eventually transforms your life. This is a paramount principle that deserves its own chapter. So let's continue on to learn how to activate the power of God's Word to transform who you are.

4

YOU ARE WHAT YOU SPEAK

Watch your thoughts; they become words. Watch your words; they become actions. Watch your actions; they become habits. Watch your habits; they become character. Watch your character; it becomes your destiny.

—UNKNOWN

LOSING WEIGHT, LEARNING something new, spending less, and getting organized top the list of Americans' most popular resolutions for a new year.[1] No doubt self-betterment in subjects such as health, finances, or managing stress is a noble goal. But issues in these areas are all too often mere symptoms of an underlying spiritual condition related to whom or what we each believe we are—our identities. Consequently, we use money, education, work, and a host of other superficial means dictated by pop culture to define ourselves, measure our successes, and steer our own destinies.

Satan loves to trap us in endless cycles of strategies for self-improvement without ever addressing the root issue. In doing so, he keeps us on a treadmill chasing a dangling carrot. We consistently exert much effort but get virtually nowhere. We work tirelessly to climb the ladder of success, to look better in certain clothes, or to be liked by more people only to feel just as empty, alone, and insignificant as before. When those don't live up to our expectations, we go in search of yet another regimen through which we might find purpose and meaning.

Ultimately the devil's strategy is to fill our minds with other voices that detract from the voice of truth that identifies us in Christ. Magazines present a certain way to look to be considered beautiful or handsome. Social media implies that a certain number of friends makes you somebody. Net worth is the measuring stick by which society quantifies success. Certain activist groups are extremely effective at pigeonholing people into their brand based on a feeling or an emotion.

Some people see themselves through the lens of the past. I emphatically understand this. As someone who was excessively shy during childhood and adolescence, it was hard for me to make friends or excel in the extracurricular activities from which many of my peers got their sense of worth. From almost day one of kindergarten I was identified as a "reject" and some other humiliating labels.

Needless to say, my sense of identity was skewed according to how I felt: alone, timid, rejected, and not good enough. Because I had nothing positive on which to build my confidence, these feelings only perpetuated more of these feelings throughout much of my adolescence and early adult life. For too many years, Satan used these voices from the past to hold me back.

Do you feel that you are alone? Rejected? A victim? A mistake? A horrible person? Unlovable? Unattractive? Unsuccessful? Inadequate? Not worthy? Insecure? Consider the source of any one of these negative feelings. They all are founded in some voice from the past or the present that is being used to tell you who you are. They are simply the devil's arguments based on a collection of false evidence he is using to prove his case. But you are the only one who will believe his prosecution. As I will demonstrate below, God's mind is already made up about you. And there is no changing that.

The Source of True Identity

I love to preach a message about the source of true identity. I call it "The Voice of Truth." I first illustrate the source of false identities by writing some of the feelings I mentioned above on a large flip chart. The people watch as I fill the page with negative descriptors that often lie at the foundation of who we believe we are.

Then I teach through a profound revelation that the Lord gave me a few years ago. I call it "The Two Transactions of the Cross." Let me explain.

The greatest extent to which most of us have experienced the cross is at salvation. In this moment we recognize our faults and identities as sinners. We understand that it was on the cross that Jesus took our sin and shame on Himself. All those things scribbled on that flip chart were crucified there, and thus we are forgiven. This is what the first part of 2 Corinthians 5:21 assures: "For our sake he made him to be sin who knew no sin." Certainly this is an essential experience in order to be born again. But giving Jesus our former identity of "sinner" is only one half of living the Christian life.

Too many Christians live in misery and defeat long after they are born again. I know I did! Perhaps you might even admit that thirty years ago you came down to some altar singing that old Billy Graham crusade classic "Just as I Am," but you felt as if you left the service the same as you were before. Hear this: to remain stuck in old habits or negative thinking patterns and to white-knuckle it until Jesus comes back is not the life that Jesus died to give you!

God revealed to me that most Christians never experience the victory that is available simply because they haven't taken the second transaction of the cross. This is the second part of 2 Corinthians 5:21: "so that in him we might become the righteousness of God." In other words, after we give our former identity of "sinner" to Jesus, we must then see ourselves in His identity, as righteous.

With this, I tear off the page of the flip chart and rip it into pieces to demonstrate that those old identifiers are gone—they were canceled and crucified at the cross (Col. 2:14). This includes past mistakes and struggles *and* the things people have said about us— all the "evidence" the enemy has used to lie to us about who we are.

Behind the torn off page is something beautiful. It is another page, prefilled with new descriptors based on the identity of Christ:

- I am a child of God (Gal. 3:26).
- I am new person (2 Cor. 5:17).
- I am the righteousness of God (2 Cor. 5:21).
- I am loved unconditionally (Rom. 8:38–39).
- I am complete (Col. 2:9–10).
- I am God's masterpiece (Eph. 2:10, NLT).

These statements are just six of the many scriptures God gives to describe your identity in Christ. These are who you truly are!

It is not difficult to notice that these attributes are polar opposites of the old ones. And the way you are identified by these proclamations is completely different as well. While the old identifiers are largely based on things you have done or have experienced, your new identity has nothing to do with anything you have done or experienced. You don't achieve these out of your own merits or striving. You aren't accepted because you met the company sales goal for the month, nor are you complete because you finally found someone who makes your heart flutter. You aren't a certain identity because you have struggled with a particular feeling or emotion. No, who you are in Christ is made up of the qualities of His image that you get to call your own simply because of His effort and striving at the cross. It is the result of *His* finished work, not yours.

Jesus's Identity Crisis

Even Jesus wasn't immune to the devil's attacks on His identity. In fact, the first confrontation Jesus faced when He launched His public ministry revolved around doubts about who God said He was and what God said He had.

Matthew's Gospel records that Jesus inaugurated His ministry by being baptized by John the Baptist. And as one would expect at a baptism for the Son of God, it didn't go as usual. Just as Jesus came up from under the water, Matthew recalled that "suddenly the heavens were opened to [Jesus] and he saw the Spirit of God descending like a dove and alighting on him" (Matt. 3:16). While that is unusual enough, what happens next is even more fascinating. A voice from heaven then declared, "This is my Son, the Beloved, with whom I am well pleased" (Matt. 3:17).

Most readers today don't get the full meaning of what happened there, but certainly the Jewish people of that day did. The four hundred years preceding Jesus's birth are known as "the silent years." This is the time between the history of God's people recorded in the Book of Malachi and that recorded in the Gospel of Matthew, when no prophets were speaking on God's behalf. Those years weren't completely silent, however, because a new phenomenon began to take place known as the *bath kol*, or "the heavenly voice." According to Jewish sources, this voice would occur from time to time, not to give new revelation, but to testify to an individual's holiness and identity.[2]

The "voice from heaven" at Jesus's baptism is a *bath kol*, used by God to confirm three things about Jesus's identity: He is God's Son, God loves Him, and God is pleased with Him.

We shouldn't be surprised that immediately after this remarkable Word from God, Jesus was questioned about it. You have likely experienced the same. Just after receiving a prophetic Word, reading a scriptural promise, or getting assurance in your heart about something God says to you, the devil comes with his all-too-common question, "Did God really say that?" And in Jesus's weakest moment, after being famished from fasting for forty days, this is precisely how the devil questioned him.

Take a look at the first statement Satan made to Jesus during His temptation in the wilderness. "*If* you are the Son of God...," the devil questioned (Matt. 4:3). Satan's first attack was a direct counter to the first words spoken by God about who Jesus is: "This is my Son" (Matt. 3:17). The devil knew that if He could get Jesus to doubt who He was, then He could get Jesus to give up

His authority. And Satan sure gave it his best shot. In all, Satan confronted Jesus three times. Let's explore the clever ways he did it and how to respond when he tries these same schemes with you.

"Prove yourself!"

Satan coupled his questioning of Jesus's identity by attempting to make Jesus prove that He is who God said He is. "If you are the Son of God, command these stones to become loaves of bread," he taunted (Matt. 4:3). In other words, Satan implored Jesus, "Do something to prove yourself!" But Jesus didn't need to prove Himself; God's Word was enough. He is God's Son regardless of what He does, simply because God said so! Jesus didn't reason with the devil, He simply countered by declaring God's Word that assures it was not bread that sustained Him, but "every word that comes from the mouth of God" (Matt. 4:4).

Indeed, it was God who declared Jesus to be His Son; He needed nothing more to sustain and prove that. And so it is for you. Though the devil would like to wear you down by getting you to try, there is nothing you can do to prove God's love for you. You are loved because God says that you are loved. Nothing you achieve and nothing in this world will uphold you in the way that God's spoken Word will.

"Here's the truth…"

With nothing in Jesus's past to use as evidence against Him, the devil then resorted to using the *truth* of Scripture, albeit in a twisted way. In his second temptation Satan said to Jesus, "If you are the Son of God, throw yourself down; for it is written, 'He will command his angels concerning you,' and 'On their hands they will bear you up, so that you will not dash your foot against a stone'" (Matt. 4:6).

Here Satan attempted to use the truth of Psalm 91 to taunt Jesus. But he conveniently left off the last part, which is the promise that Jesus would have authority over Satan.

You will tread on the lion and the adder, the young lion and
the serpent you will trample under foot.

—PSALM 91:13

Here again Jesus quoted Scripture back at Satan: "It is written,
'Do not put the Lord your God to the test'" (Matt. 4:7).

The enemy will sometimes confront you with truth too. He
will tell you about things that you have done in the past in order
to convince you that you are too far gone to be of any use in the
future. But the deception in his truth is that he always leaves out
the hope. God declares that in Christ "everything old has passed
away; see, everything has become new!" (2 Cor. 5:17). The devil
can bring up the truth of your past all he wants, but it will never
change the fact that God declares you are brand new.

"These *things* will define you."

A surely frustrated Satan tried one more tactic on Jesus. He
took him to the top of a high mountain and showed him all the
kingdoms of the world and their splendor. "All these I will give
you, if you will fall down and worship me," the devil offered (Matt.
4:9). To this I frequently ask, "Who was he kidding?" Obviously
only himself. Jesus already owned everything; there was nothing
that Satan could give him. But in this we also hear Satan try to
suggest that it is the things of the world and "their splendor" that
define Jesus as King. By now Jesus had enough. "Away with you,
Satan!" He commanded. "For it is written, 'Worship the Lord
your God, and serve only him'" (Matt. 4:10).

Jesus didn't need things to define His identity. God had already
simply but powerfully declared Him to be His Son, the beloved,
in whom He was well pleased. No kingdoms of the world, glitz,
or glamour could add to the reality of God's Word.

Don't fall into the devil's trap of associating possessions or promotions with significance or acceptance. These will only cause
you to fall down and worship these idols; they won't give you an

ounce of worth. God assures, "My grace is all you need" (2 Cor. 12:9, NLT).

The Steps of Life Transformation

Satan knows that the greatest hindrance to our being powerfully used by God to tear down his strongholds is us *believing* that we aren't good enough, that God doesn't love us, or that God is not pleased with us. That is it. Nothing else can take away your authority like insecurity about who you are.

A popular quote offers a profound insight into what ultimately affects our destinies—either negatively or positively.

> Watch your thoughts; they become words. Watch your words; they become actions. Watch your actions; they become habits. Watch your habits; they become character. Watch your character; it becomes your destiny.[3]

As we explored in the previous chapter, the outcome of your life is ultimately influenced by what begins in your mind, by what you believe. A single thought can have a viral effect and take over other aspects of your life, ultimately transforming who you are, for better or for worse.

Here's an illustration of the steps of this life transformation.

1. Thought: "You failed at that endeavor; you will never succeed at anything. You might as well quit."

2. Words: "I am a failure. This will never work out."

3. Actions: Feeling sad; walking with head held low with no confidence; quitting too early; isolating yourself from other people.

4. Habit: Being afraid of ever taking a risk again; staying within a comfort zone.

5. Character: Being known as mediocre.

6. Destiny: A defeated life that never realizes its full potential.

As you can see, a negative thought that is entertained for too long and then spoken from your mouth has a domino effect to fundamentally change you. In fact, anytime you confess, "I am _____" (fill in the blank with a negative feeling, symptom, or situation), the devil then succeeds in chipping away at your confidence in Christ, changing your behaviors, developing wrong habits in you, skewing your character, and altering your destiny.

Thankfully, just as negative thoughts and words affect your perception about who you are, so positive truths have amazing power to do the same. Paul said that we shut down Satan's mind games by taking negative thoughts captive to God's Word (2 Cor. 10:4–5). In other words, if Satan says, "You are worthless," replace that thought with the truth of God's Word and take it through the steps of life transformation.

1. Thought: "For we are God's masterpiece. He has created us anew in Christ Jesus, so we can do the good things he planned for us long ago" (Eph. 2:10, NLT).

2. Words: "I am God's masterpiece."

3. Actions: Walking with joy; making bold moves; encouraging others with your confidence.

4. Habit: Standing back up even if you fall; letting mistakes and the words of other people roll off your back.

5. Character: Being known as positive and uplifting; being seen as one who does not give up.

6. Destiny: A victorious life not swayed by circumstances or opinions.

Compare the two tracks of life transformation. The one that begins with negative thoughts and negative words ends in defeat. The one that counters negativity with the truth of Scripture and declares it accordingly enjoys a fulfilled, victorious life. It is a life not influenced by circumstances or opinions but founded on the reality: "I am God's masterpiece."

A New Habit

What kind of situation or emotion do you find yourself struggling with right now? Are you doubtful, fearful, or insecure? Are you burned out from striving to reinvent yourself? There is much truth in this old adage: "Insanity is doing the same thing over and over again and expecting different results."[4] If the same ol' same ol' isn't giving you the fulfillment and transformation you expected, it is time to change course.

Yes, it is time to break from the pattern of the world and take up the pattern of the Word. It is time to put into practice what God told Joshua to do for success and what the Book of Psalms assures is the means of refreshment: to *keep* the Word running through your mouth. Indeed, it is time to activate the power of God's Word in your life through a *habit* of speaking it aloud.

I cannot overemphasize the concept of speaking Scripture as a regular practice. Returning to Paul's analogy of the spoken Word of God as a sword, I want to point out that the spoken Word of God certainly can be used to block incoming assaults during battle. But why wait until you are under attack? When you proactively speak Scripture even in the good times, you stand in a position of victory, waving the sword offensively, threatening any would-be attackers, and warning them to stay back.

A habit of speaking Scripture is also the key to lifelong transformation. It begins to change your life through a mind-renewing cycle: speak, hear, internalize (think upon), and repeat.

This mind-renewing cycle is ultimately what Paul instructed. That is, the way to build confidence and faith in the truth of God's Word is to consistently hear the truth of God's Word so that it changes your thinking and then changes your life.

> So then faith comes by hearing, and hearing by the word of God.
> —ROMANS 10:17, MEV

The easiest, most effective way to consistently hear God's Word is to speak it yourself. This brings us back to the concept of a confession, which is what I have employed in my life to see substantial transformation. I assure you that my journey out of timidity didn't happen overnight or by merely wishing my fears and insecurities away. No, it came through the regular practice of confessing the truth of God's Word about who I am and what I have in Christ. I had to adopt a new "I am..." so that I no longer acted on the belief that "I am shy; I am rejected; I am afraid." Real transformation happened after my old pattern of thinking and speaking was completely intercepted and replaced with the truth of God's Word:

- "I am not timid, but I have power, love, and a sound mind" (2 Tim. 1:7).

- "I am chosen, accepted, and adopted into God's family" (Eph. 1:11–12).
- "I have the Holy Spirit, so, I am not a slave to fear" (Rom. 8:15).

You will notice that each of these confessions is not a word-for-word quotation of the verse on which it is based. And that is OK. This isn't about reciting memorized lines but earnestly confessing truths founded on God's Word.

I strongly advise that you ask the Holy Spirit to lead you to scriptures that counter whatever situation or emotion you face. Then personalize the scriptures into confessions that you keep with you. Finally, speak them over yourself throughout the day, as often as necessary. This will help you begin to genuinely believe what you confess. You must *identify* with God's Word in order for it to change your *identity*.

PART TWO

STRATEGIC DECLARATIONS TO DEFINE YOUR IDENTITY AND PURPOSE

5

"GOD CHOSE ME"

God decided in advance to adopt us into his own family by bringing us to himself through Jesus Christ. This is what he wanted to do, and it gave him great pleasure.

—EPHESIANS 1:5, NLT

ONE MORNING DURING my devotions I read the words Jesus used to teach His disciples about producing fruit and loving one another. Out of all the wisdom in His instructions, one statement especially stood out:

"You did not choose me but I chose you."

—JOHN 15:16

Perhaps it was the timing. I had just launched into my own ministry and was feeling very insecure about it. But in this moment Jesus's words jumped off the page and spoke very personally to me. "I chose you," I heard Him whisper.

Hearing Jesus assure me with the words *I chose you* was like a healing salve to my emotions. These three little words suddenly unpacked themselves and gave life to my weary self. They affirmed that although others had rejected me in the past, God chose me from the beginning. They confirmed God's call on my life, easing my apprehension about whether people would accept me in the ministry. With this I quickly took these words and personalized them into a declaration: "God—chose—*me*!" The magnitude of the simple but profound truth of being chosen by God was a foundation on which I built confidence for ministry. Today it still gives me the courage to keep on keeping on.

I have come to learn that I am rarely alone in my struggles. As I travel and minister, I repeatedly hear from both men and women of every age with similar uncertainties. Many people are convinced that they are accidents or mistakes and are therefore unwanted, unneeded, or undesired. I know too well how these insecurities affected my life, which is why I believe God has called me to set the record straight.

The Growing Issue of Insecurity

Begin to observe the people in your classroom, in your office, at the store, or in your church. Look at how they walk. Listen to how they talk. You will likely see one of two ways in which most hold themselves: head held low and quiet or flashy and loud. While these seem to be two very different postures, both are often rooted in the same insecurity—fear of rejection. The one who holds her head low does so because she has never had anything authentic to give her identity and confidence. In fact, she has likely experienced intense rejection in the past and is afraid of being rejected again. She therefore doesn't engage with anyone or anything in life. The one who is boisterous might have the opposite experience. He has become accustomed to people liking him for his abilities or his stuff. He therefore believes he must continue to project a flashy image to remain accepted.

These outward manifestations are the product of a society that has run amok. Sure, people of all generations have faced rejection. Kids have always been cruel to one another. People have always selected friends based on superficial characteristics such as looks or abilities. But the rejection many face today is much deeper than being passed over for a promotion or chosen last for a team. Think about the influences of these modern issues on people in our society:

- Increased divorce rates leave the other spouse feeling unwanted and the children betrayed.

- Increased births outside of marriage leave children believing they are unplanned and undesired mistakes.

- Modern science intends to show that there is neither a Creator nor a purpose to life; we are all just accidents of evolution.

- Secular culture accepts individuals based on their success, which is defined by a person's financial situation, career, or the number of social media contacts. If you don't achieve, you don't measure up.

Don't be naive about the unique challenges that pervade our culture. Many of the effects from these issues aren't simply outgrown. Often they are identity shapers with intense power to skew our beliefs about ourselves. It is therefore increasingly imperative that we look to God's Word as a solid foundation on which to build godly confidence and a healthy self-image.

Why Would God Choose Me?

I regularly hear people ask, "Why did God create people?" Certainly it is not because God needed us; He is not codependent. His security and well-being are not affected by anything we provide. No, God is self-sufficient, which means that He is complete and lacks nothing.

Second, God didn't create us because He was lonely. At the time of creation, when God spoke humankind into existence, He said, "Let *us* make humankind in *our* image, according to *our* likeness" (Gen. 1:26). God the Father was in relationship with His Son and His Holy Spirit. He definitely wasn't without company.

Finally, God didn't even need to be worshipped. Unlike some of us, God doesn't have a "love tank" that needs to be filled with words of affirmation, acts of service, or gifts. We worship God and give Him these things out of gratitude for who He is, not because He needs them to remain emotionally stable.

The answer to why God created us is fairly simple actually. God created us because He desired a family. While most of us want a family so that we don't spend the rest of our lives alone, God's desire was pure and not self-motivated. God simply wanted a family to whom He could fully express His unconditional love.

I can imagine that before the creation the Father conferred with His Son and His Spirit and said, "Let's start a family to share our love with." And He did. The Bible gives us a glimpse into this.

> Even before he made the world, God loved us and chose us in Christ to be holy and without fault in his eyes. God decided in advance to adopt us into his own family by bringing us to himself through Jesus Christ.
> —EPHESIANS 1:4–5, NLT

When I read this verse, I nearly erupt with spontaneous praise. Ponder the incomprehensible implications of what it says:

- God saw you before He made the world. Long before you were news to your parents, you were the apple of God's eye.
- God hasn't loved you just since you became a Christian, since you "got it all together," or even since you were born. No, God has *always* loved you, during everything you have been through, even before time began.
- God chose you to be set apart (holy), and He chose to see you without any faults.
- God decided, "I want _____ (fill in your name) to be a part of My family forever!"
- Through Jesus, God went to great lengths to ensure your adoption. Nothing is going to take you out!

That God adopted us adds even more significance to our place in His family. By definition, *adoption* means that parents choose someone not their own to be taken as their own and to share in the heritage and the legal rights of the family. An adopted child isn't a half child or a stepchild, but a child who is completely part of the family, the same as if he or she were a biological son or daughter.

Of course, adoption isn't without risks. The National Infertility & Adoption Education Nonprofit acknowledges on its Creating a Family website that "adoption is a leap of faith...because [children] have had experiences before coming into your home."[1] Because of the possible complications, this organization advises adoptive parents to ask serious questions to determine whether they and the child are a good match for each other. This includes in-depth scrutiny into the pasts of the biological parents, and for an older child, behavioral indicators such as his or her ability to make friends.[2]

Many of us have had plenty of negative experiences prior to joining God's family. Some come from abusive homes and parents who never knew the Lord. Others have pasts full of struggles, addictions, and regrets. Too many more have never thought of themselves as desirable to anyone. Certainly if God decided our adoptions based on an idea that "the best predictor of future behavior is past behavior," we'd all be doomed! This makes God's choice to adopt you and me all the more substantial.

God's Curious Choices

All throughout the Bible God's recruitment plan is consistent: He opts for the simple instead of the wise, the weak over the powerful, and the humble rather than the noble (1 Cor. 1:26). To be sure, God doesn't pick people like we do! Just consider some of these seemingly curious choices.

God chooses people from unthinkable situations to lead monumental movements.

When God wanted to establish a nation for Himself, He chose a man named Abraham (originally named Abram) to initiate His plan. For such a monumental task one might expect that Abraham came from a long-standing tradition of loyalty to the Lord. But that would be human wisdom. Instead, God picked a man from quite the opposite situation: Abraham came from a pagan country and a family of moon worshippers![3]

How unthinkable! Out of an idol-worshipping background, God selected Abraham as the father of a people set apart to be the envy of the world. Through Abraham came Israel. Through Israel came Moses, the man who would lead God's people from captivity into the Promised Land. Finally, out of this lineage came Jesus, who would lead us out of slavery in Satan's kingdom into the freedom of the family of God.

Abraham's story offers hope to those who feel they weren't born on the right side of the tracks or don't come from enough wealth or influence, or who feel rejected because of heritage, ethnicity, or family reputation. Remember God is masterful at bringing great things out of improbable situations. I have seen Him raise up people from families of Hinduism, Islam, or atheism to be mighty soul winners for Jesus. We can find many inspiring stories of successful business owners lifted out of generations of poverty. God certainly broke the mold with me: I am an evangelical Protestant minister from a long tradition of devout Catholics. So be encouraged! No matter your situation, God has drawn a line in the sand to say, "The old stops here. Something new starts with you!"

God chooses people with regretful pasts to be instruments of hope.

After Judas betrayed Jesus and committed suicide, the eleven remaining apostles desired to select a replacement for him. And so upon Jesus's ascension into heaven they quickly returned to

Jerusalem and huddled in a room to make their decision. There they came up with requirements for the selection of an apostle: a man who was with them during their time with Jesus's ministry, and a man who was an eyewitness to Jesus's ascension (Acts 1:21–22). From these criteria they narrowed their selections down to two men: Joseph called Barsabbas and Matthias.

Matthias was selected by the apostles in a way that we'd likely select someone today. That is, he was carefully scrutinized and chosen according to their criteria for "what makes a good apostle." But their requirements weren't the same as God's requirements. You will notice by reading the rest of the New Testament that Matthias is never again mentioned. For an individual chosen for such a prominent position, you have to wonder why the Bible does not speak of him again. I believe this is because their choice wasn't God's choice.

Several chapters later we encounter who God had in mind to replace Judas, and it was someone no one ever would have guessed. God chose Saul, a man infamously known for ravaging the homes of Christ followers and dragging them off to prison (Acts 8:3). Saul certainly didn't meet the requirements of the apostles! But God had a plan. While Saul was on his way to persecute more Christians, Jesus radically confronted him and told him to see a man named Ananias.

When God asked Ananias to meet with Saul, he was understandably hesitant. "Lord, I have heard from many about this man, how much evil he has done to your saints in Jerusalem," Ananias argued (Acts 9:13). But God's mind was made up. "Go, for he is an instrument *whom I have chosen* to bring my name before Gentiles and kings and before the people of Israel," the Lord instructed (v. 15). Amazingly, God then changed Saul's name to Paul, and he indeed became a great apostle, writing nearly 50 percent of the New Testament and bringing countless people into the faith.

Paul's legacy isn't tarnished because of his years as a persecutor of Christians, but rather his past only exalts God's work all the more. Paul serves as a real-life illustration that God sees "the end from the beginning" (Isa. 46:10). In other words, God chooses people by how they will finish, not by the condition in which they began. This is great news! God hasn't passed you over because of things that happened years ago. No, He chose you despite those things. God chose you to be His instrument that shows off His transformation.

God chooses the unlikely to be revolutionaries.

In Jesus's day, women were not very highly regarded. In truth, women were second-class citizens who were uneducated, segregated from men in worship settings, barred from public speaking, and unable to give testimony in court. Without question, nobody would have chosen a woman to make any kind of announcement, much less a world-changing one. But God did!

After His resurrection from the dead Jesus first appeared to Mary Magdalene and entrusted to her the message of all messages: "Go to my brothers and say to them, 'I am ascending to my Father and your Father, to my God and your God'" (John 20:17).

That a woman was chosen to announce Jesus's resurrection to a group of men was unthinkable enough, but there is something even more astounding here. Jesus's commission to Mary Magdalene marks the first time in John's Gospel that Jesus refers to God as "your Father" or "your God." Don't miss the significance of this! Jesus personalized God through a formerly demon-possessed woman, revealing Him as Father to all believers.

The unlikelihood of Mary Magdalene being used to announce such a revolutionary message only further exemplifies that God picks those the world considers weak, underprivileged, unworthy, and unlikely. He takes people from the back to the front; He changes the nobodies into somebodies; and He uses the unexpected to do the extraordinary.

Welcome to the Family!

No family is perfect. Not even God's. His family tree is filled with plenty of dysfunction, misfits, and broken branches. Possibly even more than yours or mine, if you can believe that! Just look into the lives of some of those listed in Jesus's lineage in Matthew 1:1–17:

- Abraham came from a culture of idol worshippers.

- Jacob deceived his father in order to steal his brother's inheritance.

- Rahab was a Canaanite prostitute.

- Ruth was a pagan foreigner.

- David committed adultery and then had the woman's husband murdered.

- Solomon turned his heart toward other gods.

These are just a handful from the list of forty! Still, despite the histories, circumstances, and scandals surrounding these unlikely people, each was uniquely chosen by God to make up the lineage of Jesus—to be in His family.

God also chose *you*. Yes, you! As we have learned, He didn't decide to adopt you because of your family history, your impeccable past, or your abilities. He didn't reject you because of a lack of those things, either. The Bible assures that the only requirement for our adoption into His family is faith in Jesus.

> But to all who received him, who believed in his name, he gave power to become children of God.
>
> —John 1:12

That's it! Before the creation of the world God made a decision about you. Think about that. He saw all the good, the bad, and the ugly of your life, yet He still desired for you to be a part of His family. What's more, He sent His Son, Jesus, to suffer the excruciating pain of the cross to ensure that you could come into

His family. No worldly rejection can measure up to the truth about the lengths God went to choose you.*

#ActivateTheWord

God chose me!

I am not an accident; I am not a mistake. Even before the world began, God desired to have me in His family. Regardless of where I am from or what I have done, because of Jesus, I am a child of God!

6

"I AM LOVED UNCONDITIONALLY"

*[Nothing] will be able to separate us from
the love of God in Christ Jesus our Lord.*

—ROMANS 8:39

KARL BARTH IS considered one of the most renowned theologians of the twentieth century. His influence on the study of God is so significant, in fact, that he is sometimes referred to as the Einstein of theology.[1]

People may debate Barth's doctrine, but there is no arguing that he had plenty to say. His most famous work, *Church Dogmatics*, covers the breadth of theology from creation to redemption in more than six million words.[2] His depth of knowledge, sometimes riddled with controversy, attracted audiences in whatever esteemed institutions he lectured throughout the world.

One of the most famous stories about this man of great intellect is also one of the most endearing. Toward the end of Barth's career, as he was closing up a lecture at the University of Chicago, someone stood up to ask, "What is the most important insight to God you have ever discovered?" At this, he paused, smiled, and replied with the words of a Sunday school song: "Jesus loves me this I know, for the Bible tells me so."[3]

Though Barth's answer sounds simple, it is as equally profound as any complex doctrine he ever espoused. Maybe that is because the concept of God's love is often hard to comprehend. Over the years countless books and sermons have tried to explain what God's love looks like, what it feels like, who God loves, and on what basis God loves someone.

Often our thoughts about God's love are handicapped by how we have observed love in our own lives. So we can't fully fathom a love that transcends self-interest, conditions, and even time itself. On a daily basis we think questions such as the following:

- What must I do to earn God's love?
- Does God still love me after I have _____ (fill in the blank with something you have done)?
- Who could love a person like me?
- How long do I have before God stops loving me?

Certainly these questions aren't influenced by anything the Bible says about God's love. Think about the truth we explored in the previous chapter: "Even before he made the world, God loved us and chose us in Christ" (Eph. 1:4, NLT). Speaking through the prophet Jeremiah, God said this about His people:

I have loved you, my people, with an everlasting love.

—JEREMIAH 31:3, NLT

Don't miss what God is saying here: He loves us with a love that can't be measured by time. He loved you well before you were born—even well before the world began. Amazingly, God promises that He loved you before you made any mistakes or had a chance to earn His love, and He loves you after you made mistakes and had a chance to lose His love. Yes, God's love for you never ends!

Correcting Our Skewed Views of God

I often talk about my religious upbringing and how it affected my view of God. To be fair, I don't recall being directly taught this, and the denomination might take issue with what I am about to say. Nonetheless, years of walking into a cold, dim sanctuary and having to perfectly memorize certain prayers and gestures shaped my view of God as distant and critical. I felt as if God was in heaven keeping a checklist of whether or not I kneeled for the proper length of time, appeared reverent enough during communion, or knew all the recited prayers. I believed God was dissatisfied with me after any failure on my part.

Some of you from similar backgrounds are nodding your heads in agreement because you can relate to these same feelings. But I am not putting the blame on any single person, event, or religious institution. Ultimately this is the devil's work. He uses whatever means will achieve his goal to erode confidence in God's love. For some he uses religious tradition. For others he uses abuses of the past or struggles in the present.

In a world laden with scandals and disaster, many people live their lives blaming those things on God, which results in a skewed concept of who He is. Recently a highly regarded study conducted by two sociology professors at Baylor University uncovered a saddening find: nearly three out of every four Americans view God as furious, critical, or distant.[4] I have simplified each of these beliefs down to some thoughts about God that I know you will recognize.

"I am afraid that God is going to get me back."

The study found that 31 percent of Americans believe that God is an authoritarian who is angry with humankind and ready to punish us at any time.[5] To be sure, this isn't anything new. This "God-is-mad" belief is what Adam and Eve held after they succumbed to Satan's temptation and took a bite of the forbidden fruit. Rather than seek God's forgiveness and move on, they hid from God out of fear of what He would do (Gen. 3:10).

People who believe similarly to Adam and Eve frequently say things such as, "That tornado was God's judgment on that town" or "God must have afflicted me with this issue because I made a mistake." What an awful way to live! These people live paranoid, and all too often they try to stay away from God out of fear of how and when He might punish them for yesterday's mistakes.

The solution to overcome the fear of God's anger is found by looking at the cross. Two thousand years ago God's wrath was satisfied once and for all as Jesus so selflessly took the punishment for sin that you and I deserve. Today God isn't trying to afflict you with His wrath; He is trying to woo you to Jesus by directing your focus to the love He poured out at Calvary. Furthermore, because you now know that God chose you to be a part of His family, it is safe to say that He isn't trying to scare you away!

"I must work hard to earn God's love."

"Critical" and disengaged is how 16 percent of Americans think of God.[6] Ultimately this is the belief that God sits in heaven critiquing your every action. To gain any kind of favor with God, these people believe they must earn it by working harder for Him.

Here again, the idea that we must work to impress God is nothing new. This is precisely what a woman named Martha tried to do when Jesus came to visit her home. The Gospel of Luke records that rather than being enamored in the company of Jesus, Martha busied herself with tasks, essentially saying, "Look at me, Jesus, and all I'm doing for you!" But Jesus wasn't impressed. Without mincing words, He indicated that it would be better for Martha to forget the to-dos and simply enjoy His presence (Luke 10:41–42).

In today's world it is hard to break the notion that we must perform to achieve. And as it was with Martha, working to impress God is often the extent of our relationships with Him. I especially see this in ministers who should know better. We think God is impressed by how many churches we plant, the number of people in our seats, or the number of books we write. It is wonderful to work in ministry and to see your work be used to help people. But don't be fooled: all your effort doesn't add one iota of significance to your value or to how much God loves you. His love is a free gift that is lavished on you simply because you are His child, not because you have earned it.

"Why did God allow this? I must have done something wrong."

Sadly, 24 percent of Americans believe that God is distant and disinterested in their everyday lives.[7] For too many this belief is deeply rooted in the idea that God has betrayed them because of something they have done.

When you read through the Old Testament, you will notice some extreme differences in Israel's thoughts about God. When all was well, they predictably praised Him for His attention to their needs. But during their time of exile, when their people were scattered, their temple was defiled, and their enemies had gained an upper hand, they quickly complained of God's absence. We can observe this in the arrangement of the Book of Psalms, which contemporary scholars believe reflects Israel's history.[8] By book two (Psalms 42–72), we begin to notice more grumbles, such as, "I say to God, my rock, 'Why have you forgotten me?'" (Ps. 42:9).

To believe that turmoil and trouble are the result of God abandoning you is foolish thinking. And that is precisely how the psalmist responds to accusations about God's absence: "Only fools say in their hearts, 'There is no God'" (Ps. 53:1, NLT). To put it into modern words, it is ridiculous to believe that God has abandoned you!

Unfortunately, most of us can admit that we have been tempted to believe God has forgotten about us. When opportunities begin to slow, some people believe it is because God has put them on a shelf and walked away. When finances get tight, others are afraid it is because they have somehow let down God and He has removed His blessing. These are lies! The Bible assures that God is always with you and is there to get you through times of great trial (Ps. 23:4).

The Enormity of God's Love

The belief that God is mad or critical or that He has abandoned you is nothing but the devil's propaganda. These aren't characteristics of God; they are characteristics of Satan! Ascribing his characteristics to God is one of the enemy's slickest tricks because it allows him to remain under the radar while God is blamed for everything. Don't fall for it! The truth about God is radically different from any of this.

> Whoever does not love does not know God, for God is love.
> —1 JOHN 4:8

God is love. This is mind-boggling to think about because most of us view love in the ways reflected by some of the dictionary's definitions:[9]

1. affection based on admiration, benevolence, or common interests
2. attraction based on sexual desire

Notice how these definitions describe *love* as "based on" something. This is another way to say that love is earned or some kind of a "you scratch my back; I will scratch yours" deal. It also suggests that love is felt as an intense euphoric feeling. The problems with these definitions are that they define *love* in ways that are fleeting. Love is not a deal to be kept, nor is it an emotion that comes and goes. And certainly neither of these reflect God's character.

To more fully comprehend the enormity of God's love, you must scratch what you have ever known about love and renew your mind according to how it is expressed by God in Scripture. In doing so, you will also begin to understand how it is possible for God to love you.

God's love is unwavering and enduring.

I marvel at the faithfulness of God's love, especially when His people are anything but faithful to Him. Perhaps the best illustration of this is seen through His determined commitment to His people Israel. After He miraculously rescued Israel from the clutches of Egyptian slavery and bore with them through a forty-year excursion to the Promised Land, Israel had a penchant for questioning God's promises and turning to idols. Their relationship with God turned so cold, in fact, that He finally gave them a certificate of divorce (Jer. 3:8). To be sure, divorce was never God's idea, but out of love, He was willing to give His people what they had already chosen in their hearts.

Even after the Israelites' total betrayal, God continued to give opportunities for Israel to come back. Just a few verses after issuing the certificate of divorce, God beckoned, "Return, O faithless children...I will take you...and I will bring you to Zion" (Jer. 3:14). These aren't the words of someone happy to wash His hands of a relationship. No, these are the words of a lovesick God offering forgiveness to a people who had already used up their share of forgiveness.

God put up with so much more than you or I would tolerate. But eventually His enduring love won the day and His bountiful mercy recaptured the hearts of His people. "O give thanks to the LORD, for he is good; for his steadfast love endures forever," the people proclaimed (Ps. 106:1). These sentiments out of the mouth of a once wayward people give us a glimpse into the depths of God and His love: He is faithful and unwavering, He loves even when love is not reciprocated, and He believes the best in people, especially when they are at their worst.

God's love is self-sacrificing.

The most widely quoted verse of the Bible is also one that vividly reveals the greatest lengths of God's love.

> For God so loved the world that he gave his only Son, so
> that everyone who believes in him may not perish but may
> have eternal life.
>
> —JOHN 3:16

That God "gave His only Son" to the world is proof that God's love was never meant exclusively for just one people group but was to be showered on His entire creation. Take note of the word *world*. In Greek it is *kosmos*, from which we derive our similar word to describe the universe. *Kosmos* is an all-encompassing word, which means that God so loved *all* His creation that He gave His only Son.[10]

To more fully understand the depths to which God loves, you must envision into what He sent His Son. Motivated by love, God sent Jesus to leave the brilliance of heaven to become a human being (Phil. 2:7). In human form Jesus endured every trial and tribulation known to people (Heb. 4:15). Then finally Jesus voluntarily suffered the ultimate punishment of being brutally mutilated on a cross.

Adding to the magnitude of the cross is that Jesus endured it for the very people who put Him there *and* for people who had yet to know Him. Paul boasted that this single act is the greatest evidence that God loves us:

> But God proves his love for us in that while we still were
> sinners Christ died for us.
>
> —ROMANS 5:8

Think about this! Jesus died for you before you had any chance to do anything that deserved it. He chose you well before you ever could have chosen Him and well after you chose other things besides Him. What could be more self-sacrificing? The cross is not merely proof of God's love for you, but it is the ultimate demonstration of it. Envision those arms of grace stretched out across that rugged, splintery cross, exhibiting just how long, how high, how wide, and how deep God's love is for you.

God's love is unconditional.

Think about some of what we just reviewed.

- Through many years God remained in love when His people didn't love Him.

- Driven by love, God sent Jesus to die for the very people who rejected Him.

- Because of love Jesus gave up His life for people who had nothing to give Him in return.

What could separate us from a love that would go to those lengths? Paul answers this question with an emphatic, "Nothing!"

> For I am convinced that neither death, nor life, nor angels, nor rulers, nor things present, nor things to come, nor powers, nor height, nor depth, nor anything else in all creation, will be able to separate us from the love of God in Christ Jesus our Lord.
>
> —ROMANS 8:38–39

How amazing! What Paul depicts here is a kind of love not affected by conditions, but based solely on the fact that God is love and there is nothing that can change who He is.

Finally, it should be said that unconditional love doesn't mean that God is pleased with everything you do. But as we have learned, God's love isn't a deal, nor is it a fleeting emotion. He is not in love with you today and threatening to leave tomorrow! God's love is the most beautiful example of what true love is: unwavering, self-sacrificing, and unconditional. And this is the love with which He absolutely loves *you*!

The Cornerstone of God's Promises

I can't overemphasize how important it is not just to know *about* God's love, but to know that God loves *you*. The words we previously read from revered theologian Karl Barth ring true. *God's love for you* is the truth on which every other truth hinges.

Believing that God loves you is the cornerstone for believing God's promises. In fact, it is what the remaining declarations in this book are founded on. Because *God loves you*, you can be certain that He has great plans for you. Because *God loves you*, you can expect that He will heal and deliver you. Because *God loves you*, you can face any difficulty knowing that He will protect and take care of you. Indeed, God's love for you is the foundation of any transformation in your life.*

#ActivateTheWord
I am loved unconditionally.

God is not mad at me; He has not forgotten about me. God has always loved me, and He proved it by sending Jesus to die for me. I declare that no person, no past, and no devil can separate me from His everlasting, unconditional love!

---

*   Go Beyond the Book: Watch my short teaching titled "The One Thing the Devil Doesn't Want to Hear You Say" at www.kylewinkler.org/videos/the-one-thing-the -devil-doesnt-want-to-hear-you-say.

7

"I AM A NEW PERSON IN CHRIST"

Anyone who belongs to Christ has become a new person. The old life is gone; a new life has begun!

—2 CORINTHIANS 5:17, NLT

WHY DID COMMON fishermen instantly drop everything to follow a Jewish rabbi who claimed to be the Son of God? How does one who was once afraid to admit to knowing Jesus suddenly begin a movement that turns the world upside down? How does a persecutor of Christianity become the leading converter to Christianity almost overnight? For that matter, how does someone like me, someone who was almost cripplingly shy in youth, become someone who takes opportunities to speak to thousands? Undoubtedly your story includes its own set of wrongs turned right, "can'ts" turned into "cans," and impossibilities made possible.

Throughout the ages Christianity has been characterized by this recurring phenomenon: in the blink of an eye God completely rewires people and gives them new beginnings, new thoughts and desires, and a radical new way to live. It is these countless, unexplainable transformations that make up the story of the faith.

The Process of Metamorphosis

At the moment someone accepts Jesus as his or her Savior, something miraculous happens. The Bible assures that old things pass away and a brand-new creation emerges (2 Cor. 5:17). Biblically this process is *metamorphoō*, which is the Greek word for what we translate as "metamorphosis" or "transform."

> Metamorphosis: a change of the form or nature of a thing or person into a completely different one, by natural or supernatural means.[1]

In the natural, metamorphosis is most often illustrated by the transformation of a caterpillar into a butterfly. The stages of this extraordinary change are fascinating.

After hatching from the egg of a butterfly, a newborn caterpillar's greatest challenge is that its skin will not grow with it. Therefore, in order to continue growing, the caterpillar must continuously produce new skin and then shed the old. A fully mature caterpillar has gone through this process four times![2]

Finally, by its fifth shedding, something different happens. What once became new skin to grow into now becomes an outer shell in which the caterpillar endures a ten- to fourteen-day transformation. Inside this dark and lonely place, the caterpillar forms wings, antennae, and mouth parts, completing its metamorphosis into a beautiful butterfly.[3]

But there is more! Though fully transformed, after it breaks from its shell, the newly emerged butterfly cannot yet fly. The butterfly first must grow its wings to full size by pumping liquid from its abdomen into its wings. Then, in its last stage, the butterfly needs to exercise its "flight muscles" before it can lift off and finally live the life for which it was destined.[4]

Your Own Transformation

I am always amazed by what God provides through creation to illustrate what He does in our lives. The butterfly is a beautiful example of God's ability to completely transform the way something looks and behaves and the purpose for which it lives. This phenomenon happened the instant you accepted Jesus; that is, a supernatural metamorphosis commenced. Like the butterfly, you too became a new creation, radically changed on the outside and the inside.

You received a new "skin."

Though we don't physically shed skin, a crucial part of our process to becoming a new creation is that we do shed the old layers of the past. This is what the verse means by "old things have passed away." At salvation you were spiritually stripped of sin, mistakes, regrets, guilt, and shame—anything from the past. But God didn't leave you bare and exposed. He gave you a new covering, though one that is not your own. It is so amazing! You received the new "skin" of Jesus and were then considered "in Christ."

Perhaps the concept of being "in Christ" seems strange to you. It doesn't mean that you are physically inside of Jesus! No, Paul described it as being clothed in Christ (Gal. 3:27), which means that you are currently dressed in the identity of who Jesus is. This is pretty remarkable. Think about some of the qualities of Christ: pure, spotless, clean, and holy. As someone clothed in Christ, you are covered in those qualities (and more!).

Being in Christ also means that you don't *do* holiness or righteousness as if these are about upholding a list of requirements or even adhering to some lifestyle rules as to what to eat, drink, or wear. That is Old Testament living! Now you are *made* holy (set apart) and in right standing with God because of your position of being "in Christ" (1 Cor. 6:11, NLT). Certainly don't take this to mean that your actions are excused from consequences; you should always desire to act in ways that are pleasing to God. But as one in Christ, your standing with God isn't based on how you act or behave, but on who Jesus is.

Your new "skin" should give you plenty of reason to celebrate. Truly it is great news! With you covered in Jesus, God doesn't see the past, nor does He condemn you for it. Now God only sees the perfect, sinless life of Jesus all over you. And that is a sight more beautiful than any butterfly!

You were *re-gened*.

Throughout the New Testament this metamorphosis is also described as being "born again"—the spiritual birthing process by which you enter a new world as a new person. Theologically speaking, this is the moment when your old life dies and you are then made alive to God in Christ (Rom. 6:11). This is also known as regeneration.

From *regeneration* we get the concept of being *re-gened*. I like to use this term because it provides a great word picture for what actually happens at new birth. Being *re-gened* implies that your DNA has changed. And as we know, DNA is the carrier of all genetic information, which determines almost everything about you: hair and eye color, height, some behavioral predispositions, and so on. Your regeneration in Christ, however, doesn't just start you over with a new set of genes; you are *re-gened* with the nature of God.

> Those who have been born of God do not sin, because God's seed abides in them; they cannot sin, because they have been born of God.
>
> —1 JOHN 3:9

The Greek word for *seed* in this verse further unpacks the idea of what happens here. It is *sperma*, from which we get the word *sperm*. In other words, at your new birth, God's DNA was given to you. With this, God's DNA *re-gened* you into His family and His kingdom. Yes, God placed His nature in you so that you now contain the qualities of who He is.

Amazingly, *you contain the DNA of God!* You should speak that over yourself right now. Declare it: "I contain the DNA of God!" The enigma of this truth is that you *already have* so much of what you have been praying for. Because God is love, joy, and peace, for example, you don't need to beg Him to give you these things. But rather you simply need to activate the power of God's

Word to develop and grow what is already in you. And that is precisely what you are learning to do through this book.

A New Way to Live

How is your Christian life? Is it exciting? Is it adventurous? Is it powerful? If not, it should be! Too many people settle for a lackluster Christian life because they have only thought of their new life as a concept that affects eternity and not as something that affects today. Yes, salvation guarantees an eternity in God's presence, but Jesus also died to radically transform your everyday life. Be encouraged by some of the following transformations that give you an exciting and powerful new way to live.

You live in a new world.

Immediately upon accepting Christ, you were transferred from the grip of this world and all its trappings into the kingdom of Jesus.

> He has rescued us from the power of darkness and transferred us into the kingdom of his beloved Son, in whom we have redemption, the forgiveness of sins.
>
> —COLOSSIANS 1:13

One of the chief effects of salvation is that evil, controlling influences are severed by the power of the cross. As a new person in Christ, you were instantly taken off Satan's path of destruction and placed on God's path of abundant life. (See John 10:10.) You no longer live in a place where the past can haunt you. Old things are gone! You now live in a place of grace, where your sins aren't merely forgotten but are completely obliterated without the possibility of being brought up again (Ps. 103:12).

Finally, I want you to notice that Colossians 1:13, the verse above, doesn't say that we are transferred into heaven, but that we are transferred into the kingdom. This is significant and makes all the difference in how you live your life here and now. Jesus revealed that the kingdom is *here*. (See Luke 17:21.) And throughout the New Testament *kingdom* is equated with the powerful presence of God. As a new person in Christ, you spiritually reside in God's presence, which is governed by His power and the laws of the supernatural. Here all things are possible! Through even a simple prayer you can invade the natural world with the supernatural power of the kingdom to open blind eyes and deaf ears, heal the sick, and cast out demons. Here, you can also believe to walk in divine health and favor. Though you physically live in this world, the kingdom and all its power are just as real and are here for you to access and enjoy right now.

You have new senses.

Our physical bodies are designed with five senses: touch, sight, taste, smell, and hearing. Most of our lives are lived in reaction to these senses. And if we are honest, many of us are slaves to these, too often judging what to do or not to do solely on how we *feel*.

Certainly Christians still have feelings. But with your new birth you were given two new guides to which your physical feelings take a backseat. The first is God's Holy Spirit. Jesus promised His "Spirit of truth" would come to live inside whoever believes in Him and serve as a helper and advocate (John 16:13). The Holy Spirit will nudge you and speak to you in ways that don't make sense to your senses! He will wake you up in the middle of the night to pray. He will ask you to give your hard-earned money to a cause. He will convict you to make adjustments in your life that are sometimes uncomfortable and uneasy.

Hearing the voice of the Holy Spirit takes practice and experience. With intentionality and time you will learn to differentiate His voice from your own. But in whatever ways He leads, be assured that the Spirit's goal is never to harm you or hold you back. Because He knows the future, He guides you into the best decisions that will help you fulfill your God-given destiny.

The second guide is God's Word, which Paul instructs is useful to teach, correct, and prepare us in this new life (2 Tim. 3:16–17). The truths of God's Word serve as a "true north" when feelings point in every other direction. In my life there have been countless times when the sights and sounds of a certain situation filled me with near paralyzing fear. In these moments I had the opportunity to give in to this sense of fear and quit or to trust God's Word and press on. I can't claim to be perfect in this, but I have learned that when I trust God's Word, I am always glad I did. Coupled with the leadership of the Holy Spirit, God's Word as your guide will never lead you in a wrong direction but will always steer you toward your destiny.

You have a new way to think.

People of the world gain wisdom through experience and by observing the world. Think about many of the self-help books on the shelves—they are filled with the wisdom of doctors, counselors, and teachers who derived their knowledge from observed behaviors and patterns. This isn't all bad, but the Bible promises that the new person in Christ thinks differently and has access to greater wisdom because he or she now has the mind of Christ.

> For, "Who can know the LORD's thoughts? Who knows enough to teach him?" But we understand these things, for we have the mind of Christ.
>
> —1 CORINTHIANS 2:16, NLT

Possessing the mind of Christ gives you two major benefits. First, Christ's mind isn't restrained by logic and reason. In fact, His thoughts are often way outside of reason! I know some Christians who baffle their accountants every year because they seemingly outgive their income, yet the balance always works out in the end. Who in their natural mind would forsake sleeping in on a day off in order to sing and listen to an hour-long talk in church? Who would give up precious vacation time to fly to Africa or Haiti and risk his or her life for Jesus's name? Your seemingly "crazy Christian" desires aren't your own; they are the results of a new way of thinking according to the mind of Christ.

Having the mind of Christ also means that you have an advantage over anyone in the world because you have insight from the Creator who knows all things. God knows the best business plan. He knows the best cure. He knows the best decision for the best outcome. When I am stuck on a problem, feel confused, or am forgetful, I often activate this truth by declaring, "I have the mind of Christ." It never takes long before I stand amazed at the answers and solutions God never fails to provide. As a new person in Christ, you can—and should—do the same.

You have a new way to talk.

Perhaps one of the greatest outcomes of being a new person, in a new kingdom, with new senses and thoughts, is that you also have a new way to talk. Gone should be the days when your speech reflects the difficulties of your circumstances or the ups and downs of your feelings. Rather, Paul instructs that Christians are to speak as believers (2 Cor. 4:13). In other words, your mouth is to reflect the height of your faith.

To put this practically, there is no place for grumbling, fault-finding, or negativity. I am saddened when I hear Christians say, "I'm just playing the devil's advocate." The devil doesn't need an advocate! He does a fine job of discouraging people on his own; he certainly doesn't need your help. Instead, desire to be the Holy Spirit's advocate and speak encouraging words of faith to each other, about yourself, and over your situations.

Speaking in faith doesn't mean that you ignore reality. It simply means that instead of using your mouth to prophesy doom to that reality, you use your mouth to speak life to it. This is the whole purpose of this book. Rather than react to bad news by confessing Murphy's law—"Anything that can go wrong, will go wrong"—conform your mouth to God's Word and declare, "I believe God will turn this into something good!"

But I Don't Feel New!

Perhaps you feel a bit insecure because you don't see all these evidences of the new life active in your life. Fear not! Though we are instantly given the covering of Christ and *re-gened* with the nature of God, all the fruits of the new creation don't instantly mature all at once. Think about the newly emerged butterfly. Though it has wings, it can't immediately fly. It must first exercise its flight muscles before it is able to lift off.

As Christians we must build our faith muscles by renewing our minds according to God's Word. In fact, the Bible instructs that the renewal of the mind is absolutely essential for complete transformation.

> Do not be conformed to this world, but be *transformed* by
> the renewing of your minds.
> —ROMANS 12:2

Remember, even if you don't *feel* completely new, God's Word is more real than what you feel. The reality is that God says that you are brand new. Therefore, you must renew your mind to think and speak like it, and then you will begin to live like it.*

#ActivateTheWord
I am a new person in Christ.

I am no longer identified by past sins, mistakes, or regrets, but by the righteousness of Jesus. Because God has placed His Spirit and His nature in me, I live in the power of His presence, according to the truth of His Word, and with the mind of Christ and a mouth of faith.

---

* Go Beyond the Book: Watch my short teaching titled "Unleash the New Life Already in You" at www.kylewinkler.org/videos/unleash-the-new-life-already-in-you.

8

"GOD HAS GREAT PLANS FOR ME"

For we are God's masterpiece. He has cre-
ated us anew in Christ Jesus, so we can do the
good things he planned for us long ago.

—EPHESIANS 2:10, NLT

G OD IS PURPOSE driven. There is nothing that He considers "just for the fun of it." From small to large, everything God puts His hands on and His words and thoughts to is intentional and purposeful, even if His purposes aren't immediately clear.

I could take the rest of this book to talk about the events and people of the Bible that God set forth to bring about His plans. But the reasons for their mentions in Scripture are fairly apparent. God wouldn't include something or someone in His book if He didn't have a point to make by doing so.

What isn't so obvious to many today is the purpose for which God has brought them into existence. The modern issues we explored in chapter 5 make this all the more full blown. It is easy to understand how those born out of unplanned pregnancies might believe they are an "oops" with no purpose, or how modern science influences people to believe that we are all just accidents of evolution.

Accordingly, we should not be surprised that one in five people today struggles with depression, often rooted in feeling purposeless.[1] The relationship between these feelings and depression is so common, in fact, that successful treatment frequently involves methods to reestablish the individual's sense of purpose—things such as creating a routine, setting goals, taking on responsibilities, doing something new, or volunteering for a cause.[2] While these activities in themselves can't give someone significance, they work by helping the individual *see* and *believe* that his or her life has meaning. Here again, this all reinforces how our beliefs directly impact our lives and thus why it is essential to know and stand on the truth of God's Word.

How God Reveals His Masterpieces

In the previous chapters you learned that God chose you before the creation of the world; nothing about you came about by happenstance. To build on this, you should know that God crafted your every feature with great care *for a great reason*. Truly you are so wonderfully planned that God boasts about you as one of His masterpieces:

> For we are God's masterpiece. He has created us anew in Christ Jesus, so we can do the good things he planned for us long ago.
> —EPHESIANS 2:10, NLT

Hear this again: you are God's masterpiece. You are not God's flop, dud, or failure. You are God's work of art, His showpiece, and one of His greatest achievements—not meant merely to be admired on a shelf or a wall, but for the purpose of doing "the good things he planned."

Yes, long ago God molded you with a mission in mind! He is extremely proud of what He will accomplish through your life and how He will advance His story through you. And so day by day God chisels you to more fully uncover this masterful plan. No situation or event is beyond God's use. In fact, it is often the unlikely and unexpected circumstances that He uses to perform His greatest reveals.

God's plans are often revealed in ways no one considered.

When I stepped out into the first real endeavor with my own ministry, people laughed. I was in my midtwenties and for a handful of years had mostly served in behind-the-scenes roles. After a while a passion began to bubble up in me to share stories of God's power. I knew what God had done in my life, and I wanted people to hear and believe that He would do the same for them. With this, I decided to begin by filming and broadcasting interviews with people who had dramatically encountered God's power and transformation.

Because of my position in another ministry I was blessed with access to a TV studio where I could film. I will never forget the first interview I hosted. I invited about a dozen friends and coworkers for moral support. We readied the set just before the guest arrived, and on the screen behind me I unveiled my new logo. This is when the laughter happened! Keep in mind that at this point my friends had only ever known me as a behind-the-scenes, techy kind of person. Suddenly revealing a ministry logo probably seemed a bit pretentious to them. And certainly this kind of an up-front role was much beyond what they imagined for me.

Now, more than five years later, nobody's laughing. I stand amazed at how God moved me from a behind-the-scenes helper to more of a public figure. Though the plan continues to unfold, He uses me in ways immensely different than others thought possible. And that is what He does for so many. Through His plans for you and me, He reveals His ability to "accomplish abundantly far more than all we can ask or imagine" (Eph. 3:20).

God's plans are sometimes revealed through an accident.

History is filled with people born out of curious circumstances but whom God created with great purposes, nonetheless. Timothy, the young evangelist companion to the apostle Paul, is one of these people. His mother, Eunice, was a Jew, but his father was Greek. According to Jewish law, Jews weren't supposed to marry anyone outside of the Jewish race. Their marriage was a big no-no, and Timothy was the result.

God's plan for Timothy far superseded the scandal through which he was born. His life was crucial in helping Paul start and maintain many of Christianity's first churches. Certainly this "oops" had a large role in God's master plan.

God also has a knack for uncovering purpose even out of the events we consider to be accidents. Consider what happened to my friend Ashley. At about sixteen years old, she attended a church youth group with me, and she went on an overnight skiing adventuring with our group. But what Ashley thought was going to be merely a fun night of skiing turned out to be a destiny revealer.

About halfway through the night Ashley finally built up the courage to tackle one of the larger slopes. But as slopes sometimes do, this one tackled her, landing her in the hospital with several broken bones. Yes, the accident was unfortunate, but the outcome wasn't. Through it Ashley realized a key part of God's plan for her life was to be a health care worker. From that incident, she went on to be a firefighter, an EMT, a flight nurse, and a trauma nurse. Though Ashley isn't anyone famous, in just fifteen years she has helped thousands of people in some of the most critical situations. That God used a tumble down a hill to reveal His plan for Ashley illustrates His uncanny ability to turn a bad situation into something good (Rom. 8:28). It also shows that we are often called to people in situations and with issues similar to what we have faced.

What Is God's Plan for Me?

I could go on and on with inspiring stories of great accomplishments and all the fascinating ways God reveals His plans to people. But by now you are likely thinking, "What about me? How do I discover God's plan for me?" The great news is that it is not all that difficult to begin to sense God's will for your life, but there are a few essential steps.

Step 1: Meet with God.

The first must-do to determine God's plan is crucial: you must meet with Him. There is no way around this. You can't hear from someone without meeting with him. Time in God's presence always reveals purpose, sometimes in dramatic, instant fashion, but most often through gradual, day-to-day revelation.

The apostle Paul's conversion illustrates the dramatic. On the road to Damascus, Paul suddenly experienced a blinding, radiant light coming from the heavens, which knocked him to the ground. Suddenly in the presence of Jesus, a trembling Paul asked about his purpose. "Lord, what will You have me do?" (Acts 9:6, MEV).

Paul's encounter in the Lord's presence was the kind that immediately sets someone on a new path. I have known people to have these at the altar, on the side of the road in a car, in front of the TV, or on their pillows at night. While you can put yourself in environments that make an experience such as this more likely, they are still spontaneous and infrequent.

Your purpose will most likely be revealed through day-to-day, intentional time in God's presence, such as in Bible reading, worship, or prayer. This is how I began to discern what God wanted to do through me. While I never once heard an audible voice saying, "Kyle, do this," through time with God I felt Him plant passions within me that have never wavered.

I pray the Holy Spirit reveals Himself to you mightily and downloads God's will for you in an instant. But if that doesn't happen, don't feel left out. Find some time in each day to meet with God. Worship Him. Talk to Him. Listen to Him. The Bible promises that God draws near to those who draw near to Him (James 4:8). I assure, in time, you will feel desires bud within you that you just can't shake.

Step 2: Start moving.

When Paul asked, "Lord, what will You have me do?" Jesus replied to him with the next step in the plan—not the entire plan. He didn't say, "Paul, you will start many Gentile churches and will write nearly half of the New Testament." No, Jesus said, "Get up and enter the city, and you will be told what you are to do" (Acts 9:6). From there God revealed to Paul pieces of the plan, step-by-step as he went.

I can't think of anyone who ever received his or her entire plan from the Lord all at once. I believe God withholds some of it for a few reasons. First, if we knew everything, it might scare us. Second, God doesn't want us to find our worth in what we do. Third, and probably most important, God isn't as interested in what we accomplish for Him as He is in our building relationships of trust with Him. By revealing His plans in part, we must continuously listen for each step and trust Him to help us achieve it.

One of the greatest truths I learned early in my Christian walk is that "you can't move a parked car." Inevitably there will be times when you aren't quite sure what God wants you to do. In these moments, rather than do nothing, start to do something, and trust that the Lord will steer you from there. The Bible assures us that He will adjust and redirect your course along the way.

> The LORD directs the steps of the godly. He delights in every
> detail of their lives.
>
> —PSALM 37:23, NLT

Since the time I was eighteen years old, I knew that God called me to ministry, but I had no concept about the shape it would take. So I stepped out to try various ministries, including elementary Sunday school teaching and street evangelism. I very quickly learned that neither of those were my calling, and I moved on. To be sure, these trial experiences weren't wasted. God used it all as He guided my steps toward what I do today.

What passion has God infused in you? Preaching to the

unsaved? Teaching those in the church? Business? Government? Music? Family? Don't wait to do something until you know every detail of the plan. That will never happen! Prayerfully take a step to do something in the direction of your passion. Don't be paralyzed into inaction out of fear that you might take the wrong step. Trust that God is in control, guiding and directing your steps. Even if you do make a mistake, God will get you back on track!

Step 3: Stop comparing.

God's plan for your life may very possibly be right under your nose, but you are blind to it because you are in search of something more grandiose. When you hear, "God has great plans for you," know that *greatness* is not measured numerically. God's plans for someone are great because they uniquely achieve a desired outcome for the Lord, not because through them you will achieve fame or fortune. A great plan of God might mean raising an upstanding family, faithfully pastoring a congregation of fifty, or being a solid Christian example in your workplace. Success in God's kingdom doesn't look one particular way. It is not about how much you receive or achieve, but about being faithful and obedient with whatever measure God gives (Matt. 25:23).

We must be content with whatever role God gives us, regardless of the size. Mordecai Ham, the evangelist who led young Billy Graham to the Lord, lived with just as great of a plan as Billy. Certainly the scope of Billy Graham's ministry was far wider than Mordecai's, but it was equally significant to God. Someone had to have the role of leading Billy Graham to the Lord, which was part of God's purpose for Mordecai. And today we all celebrate his obedience. Never underestimate the enormous impact that even a seemingly small position in God's plan might have in years to come.

Ultimately realize that God gave you your strengths, talents, and passions for a reason. Build on those rather than wishing for someone else's. Your unique gifts are all part of His plan to accomplish things and to reach people that others can't.

God's Plans for You Are Intact

I can't write a chapter about God's great plans without mentioning the verse that is most commonly used to support it.

> For surely I know the plans I have for you, says the LORD, plans for your welfare and not for harm, to give you a future with hope.
> —JEREMIAH 29:11

This verse, spoken by God through the prophet Jeremiah, is often the fodder for graduation and sympathy cards. Though it is inspiring on its own, in context the verse provides a greater truth than any of the overused, cliché expressions.

The people of Israel were at their lowest, most desperate moment. Enemies ravaged their temple, and tens of thousands were scattered from their homes into foreign lands. To add to the chaos, false prophets arose that spoke winsome promises that all fell flat (e.g., Jer. 28:3). Undoubtedly God's people were on an emotional roller coaster that left them feeling jaded and hopeless.

When God's people were in these depressing circumstances, He spoke to them through Jeremiah. "I will fulfill to you my promise and bring you back to [your homeland]," He assured. "I know the plans I have for you...plans for your welfare and not for harm, to give you a future with hope" (Jer. 29:10–11).

God's words through Jeremiah perhaps weren't as sensational as what His people had heard from others before, nor did they outline the specific ways or timetable in which God would restore His people. But God's words provided the solid assurance to a weary people that He was in control, His plan was still intact, and they could trust Him to bring it to pass.

Allow God's promise to transcend time and speak to you today. He declares, "I am in control; My plan for you is intact; I will make it happen." Don't grow weary in waiting, but be expectant of what is to come. God's Word assures that He has a great plan for you. Trust that the circumstances of today will not harm you but that God will use it all to prepare you for what is ahead. Enjoy where you are on the way to where you are going.*

#ActivateTheWord
God has great plans for me!

Long ago God created me as His masterpiece for a good purpose. I trust that every day He shapes my circumstances and guides my steps to fulfill His plan. I will enjoy the journey, knowing that God is in control and that His plans for me are sure to happen.

---

* Go Beyond the Book: Watch my short teaching titled "What to Do While You Wait…on God" at www.kylewinkler.org/videos/what-to-do-while-you-wait-on-god.

PART THREE

STRATEGIC DECLARATIONS FOR **REST** AND **REFRESHMENT**

9

"I DON'T WORRY ABOUT ANYTHING"

Don't worry about anything; instead, pray about everything. Tell God what you need, and thank him for all he has done.

—PHILIPPIANS 4:6, NLT

PERHAPS NO EMOTION is more common to the human condition than fear. We all have felt it, and we know its crippling effects. But to overcome fear, we must understand what causes it.

Psychologists say that the natural progression to fear happens in three stages: worry, anxiety, and then fear.[1] The first stage—worry—is a simple thought created by a question that enters the mind, a question such as one of the following:

- Will I get hurt by this person?
- Will I have enough money to pay the bills this month?
- What if I fail in this venture?
- Where are my children right now?

Thoughts such as these put our minds into overdrive mulling over all the possible scenarios. When these questions are left unanswered, a person can slip into a state of apprehension known as anxiety. The essence of anxiety is this: when situations seem uncertain, the mind begins to search frantically for some sort of certainty. But because these questions often relate to something in the future, the mind can't find a satisfying answer. Therefore, these unresolved what-ifs lead to either occasional bursts of nervousness or a long-term sense of anxiousness and unease.

Left unchecked, one who constantly lives focused on what-ifs eventually succumbs to a lifestyle of fear. At this stage the mind believes that danger is imminent, so it seeks to protect by influencing someone to stop, give up, run and hide, or do anything *but* what is influencing the feeling of fear.

Similar to any stronghold, fear is an absolute master, making the individual a slave. This is why I believe the devil uses this process strategically against God's people. If he can lead us into fear, he knows he can paralyze us into inaction and thwart many of the blessings and opportunities God has for our lives.

Do I Just Need More Faith?

Surely you have heard someone boast that the solution to worry, anxiety, and fear is to "have faith." The idea is that faith is the opposite of fear and can simply be mustered up at will to overcome it. *Faith*, however, is defined by the dictionary as "complete trust of confidence in someone or something." [2] Its biblical definition is similar: "the evidence of things not seen" (Heb. 11:1, NKJV). In other words, both the dictionary and the Bible describe faith as confidence in a particular outcome you can't yet see. This can be either positive or negative.

Accordingly, if the answer to any of your mind's questions causes you to worry or be anxious, it is not because you don't have faith. No, the Bible teaches that we all have a measure of faith (Rom. 12:3). When you sit down on a chair, you have faith that it is going to hold you up. When you press the start engine button or turn the key in the ignition of your car, you have faith that it is going to start. You do all kinds of activities in life with no second thought because you have some amount of faith. And as Jesus assured, some amount of faith (as small as a mustard seed) is all you need to do big things (Matt. 17:20). Your faith just has to be directed in the right way.

Ultimately worry, anxiety, and fear happen because the measure of faith you do have is misplaced on the negative. Simply put, fear is faith, or the confident expectation, that something bad is going to happen. Therefore, in order to overcome it, you have to learn how to redirect your faith to positive expectations set by God's Word. While it does take time to retrain the mind accordingly, God has outlined strategies that make this entirely possible. Keep reading.

How to "Fear Not!"

The Bible is filled with stories of people who faced seemingly insurmountable situations. I am sure that the stories we read today don't do justice to convey the emotions of worry that our favorite Bible heroes faced in some of their moments. Still, these people *all* made it through the situations they likely feared—many because of a single command of God: "Be strong and courageous" (Josh. 1:9); "Do not be afraid" (Isa. 41:10); or "Do not worry about anything" (Phil. 4:6).

Perhaps the pat answer, "Fear not!" seems a bit cavalier. Is God being inconsiderate or insensitive by issuing such blanket statements? Isn't there more to overcoming these emotions than just to say, "Don't feel that way"? How is it possible to simply "not worry" when faced with such difficult circumstances such as one of the following:

- Being diagnosed with a life-threatening disease
- Discovering your spouse is cheating
- Being laid off from work
- Having children who are in trouble with the law
- Being single at thirty-five
- Listening to news reports of terrorist attacks and disasters

To be sure, none of these or the many other challenges that people face are taken lightly by God. He is not a blunt counselor whose only advice is, "Suck it up and get tough!" God is able to encourage you to "Fear not!" simply because He knows all the dirty secrets about fear and the definite ways to avoid it. Here's what God wants you to know.

Fear is often a figment of your imagination.

A famous quote often attributed to Mark Twain conveys an important insight about fear. "I have been through some terrible things in my life," Twain remarked. "Some which actually happened."[3] Twain's somewhat tongue-in-cheek comment is humorous to most of us because we realize its truth—most of what we worry about never comes to pass.

The University of Cincinnati conducted a worry-related study that gives scientific credibility to Twain's quote. Remarkably, the study revealed that a whopping 85 percent of what we fear never happens.[4] While these fears may be based on actual events, we bite our nails, lose sleep, and stress over outcomes that are nothing more than fairy tales. What a waste of precious time and energy!

Similarly, well before any study, the apostle Paul instructed that many of the fears we face are make-believe mind games, which he referred to as "imaginations" (2 Cor. 10:5, MEV). Our minds constantly make up narratives about situations by piecing together bits of factual information and then filling in the gaps with worst-case scenarios.

I once heard a riddle that profoundly illustrates the power of the mind to do this. Follow this and see what scenario your mind builds: A man left home running. He ran a little ways and turned left. He ran a little ways and turned left. He ran a little ways and turned left, and then, he ran back home. When the man returned home, there were two masked men waiting for him. Why did the man start to run and who were the masked men?[5]

Note the facts in this riddle: a man runs from home and makes three left turns before returning home, and two masked men wait for him back at home. It is likely that your mind used these facts to build a horrible situation—probably that the man was running from danger but was ultimately caught by the masked men in the end. The reality of the situation couldn't be further from this, however. And a single word of truth will undo everything your mind created. Think "baseball." Yes, the man is a batter who had hit a home run. And the two masked men are the catcher and the umpire!

Indeed, the mind is a powerful device that needs to be tamed! This is why Paul urged that the only way to combat these imaginations is to "take every thought captive to obey Christ" (2 Cor. 10:5). What this means is that when you recognize a thought that begins to cause worry, it is imperative that you immediately replace it with the truth of God's Word, such as the declarations you are learning throughout this book. Left on their own, imaginations quickly grow into full-blown, convincing stories that cripple you with fear. But when confronted with truth, imaginations are exposed for what they are—foolishness!

Your past can help build courage.

When young David went out to face the warrior Goliath, he didn't conjure up his courage from nowhere. No, David's fearlessness was rooted in God's faithfulness in his past.

Just before suiting up for battle, David recalled to Saul that as a shepherd he had struck down lions and bears to save lambs (1 Sam. 17:34–36). Because he wisely accredited his strength in these times to the Lord, he then made a sweeping faith declaration that God would also help him take down Goliath:

> The LORD, who saved me from the paw of the lion and from the paw of the bear, will save me from the hand of this Philistine.
>
> —1 SAMUEL 17:37

David's profound faith to defeat Goliath came from the expectation that God, who saved him many times before, would do it again. He had such trust, in fact, that he never gave it a second thought. With no sign of fear, he ran quickly to the battle line, launched a stone from his sling, and watched as Goliath plummeted to the ground.

Reminders of God's faithfulness in my past have been crucial for me to overcome anxiety while charging toward new frontiers in my life and ministry. At nearly every transition and risky move, I have had to look back into my history to realize, "God got me through that, and that, and that." Each time I do this, it builds my faith to declare, as David did, "I believe God will get me through this too!"

We all have a history with God. You are reading this today having survived trials you never thought you could make it through; yet here you are. You too can run quickly to the battle line to face whatever giants present themselves in your life by simply remembering God's goodness in your past. Remember, if God did it before, He will do it again. God will part those waters again. He will move those mountains again. He will heal again. He will deliver again. Hear this: God will do it again!

You can be fearless even if you don't feel fearless.

When the Lord commissioned Joshua to lead His people into the Promised Land, three times He instructed him to "be strong and courageous" (Josh. 1:6, 9, 18). Notice that God never once told him to *feel* courageous, but to *be*. There is a crucial difference here. A *feeling* is an emotional reaction based on the environment and other external circumstances often outside of one's control. This is why feelings can be so fickle. But *be* is defined as "to occupy a position or space." [6] *Being* isn't an emotional response, but rather, it is an intentional decision to take on a certain quality. In other words, we can decide to *be* strong and courageous even if we don't *feel* strong and courageous.

I am sure Joshua wasn't void of the feeling of fear. Imagine suddenly being charged to lead a large group of whining, wayward people into an unknown land that has taken forty years to get to! Furthermore, he had to get these people, along with the ark of the covenant, across the Jordan River at flood stage. To accomplish such a monumental feat, Joshua had to forge ahead despite the myriad emotions that likely tried to talk him out of his responsibilities. And he succeeded.

Comparably, anything worthwhile in my life has come by pushing through despite my feelings. Toward the beginning of my ministry experience, I was working for a megachurch in southern Florida. I had a comfortable position with good pay and benefits in a location I loved. But suddenly I felt restlessness arise in me out of a sense that a transition was about to happen, though I couldn't discern in what way.

Months later I wept in my car the day I finally realized what God was leading me to do. He wanted me to move nine hours up the road to the panhandle of Florida to help restore a ministry that had played a pivotal role in my early Christian years. Unfortunately, due to a series of missteps and bad leadership choices, this once flourishing organization was nearly burned to the ground and left in disarray. Suffice it to say, leaving the good situation I had in southern Florida to join this ministry was a risky move. And when I announced my decision, friends and family aired their concerns about the foolishness of it all.

Why would I leave one of my favorite areas of the country and a job at a well-respected church to move to a location where I didn't know anyone to work for an organization whose fate was unknown? Because God told me to do it! I could spend much time recounting all the ways God confirmed what He wanted me to do. But even all the so-called "signs" didn't erase the fear I felt in the weeks and days that led up to the move. Nonetheless, I did it. Even with shaking knees and butterflies in my stomach, I did it. I did it afraid. I did it with no idea of the outcome. But I did it. Today, a decade later, I am glad that I did. It worked out just as God promised. And I believe many were blessed because of my obedience to follow God's call despite my feelings.

When God tells you to "Fear not!" He doesn't mean that you won't feel the effects of fear. He doesn't mean that you won't experience anything that might cause worry. Ultimately God asks you to move forward by placing your faith in Him for a positive outcome even if everything around you—friends, family, or circumstances—says otherwise.

You have anytime access into God's peace.

All throughout the Old Testament, God's presence is considered the source of refuge, help, and comfort in the midst of trouble. In the New Testament, Jesus invited all who felt weary and stressed to find relief in His presence. "Come to me," He said. "You will find rest for your souls [mind, will, and emotions]" (Matt. 11:28–29).

Indeed, all who came to Jesus found restoration and refreshment from life's burdens. But this didn't end with His ascension into heaven. No, Jesus promised to send an eternal helper—His Holy Spirit—who would come to live inside every Christian (John 14:16). What this means is that the presence of God, which has always been the source of peace, is no longer something external that can come and go. But rather, the presence of God and His peace live inside of you, forever *with* you.

It is no coincidence that the Holy Spirit is referred to as the Comforter. It is certainly comforting to know that the One who created the heavens and the earth is with you and is in control. No situation in your life can take God's Spirit by surprise. Nothing is too large for the Almighty to handle. This is why Paul frequently boasted that the presence of the Holy Spirit frees God's people from fear.

The Spirit you received does not make you slaves, so that you live in fear again.

—ROMANS 8:15, NIV

For God has not given us a spirit of fear and timidity, but of power, love, and self-discipline.

—2 TIMOTHY 1:7, NLT

Because God's Spirit is with you, you have anytime access into His peace. It only takes a split second to come before God, who comforts, "Cast all your cares on Me because I care for you!" (1 Pet. 5:7).

What causes you to worry today? Is it finances? A relationship? Your children? Your safety? Your health? Whatever it is, tell God right now. He is here! Surrender your fears at His feet. When you relinquish control of trying to make everything happen, you put God in His rightful place as Lord over everything. I promise He can master your worries much better than you! So take a moment, breathe deeply, and say, "God, You are in control." Feel His supernatural peace take over and envelop your heart and mind in ways you never thought possible (Phil 4:7). Now relax! There is nothing to fear!*

#ActivateTheWord
I don't worry about anything.

I am not influenced by feelings of worry, anxiety, or fear, but I have love, power, and self-control. Because God's Spirit lives within me, I am strong and courageous. I cast all my cares on the Lord, and I know that His peace is guarding my heart and mind in Christ Jesus.

---

* Go Beyond the Book: Watch my short teaching titled "The Cure for Fear" at www .kylewinkler.org/videos/the-cure-for-fear.

10

"I ENJOY MY LIFE"

This is the day that the LORD has made;
let us rejoice and be glad in it.

—PSALM 118:24

MOST PEOPLE LIVE in one of two places. Plagued by guilt, shame, and regret, some spend much of their time in the past, licking wounds, nursing hurts, or reliving mistakes. Others spend much of their time in the future, worrying about what is ahead, trying to resolve uncertain situations, or dreaming about opportunities and success.

While the past and the future are both very different places, neither actually exists. The past is merely a memory—a picture or video locked in the mind that is no longer tangible. The future, on the other hand, is nothing more than a fantasy—an imagination based on hopes, dreams, or even fears. But neither is it tangible. Neither the past nor the future can actually be lived in, yet so many of us try to live there and, in so doing, rob ourselves of the enjoyment of today. A renowned quote sums this up the best:

> Yesterday is history. Tomorrow is a mystery. Today is a gift.
> That is why it is called the present.[1]
>
> —ALICE MORSE EARLE

Indeed, *today*—right now—is a present from God. But do you appreciate it as such? Take time to think about what is happening in your life in this moment. What is your attitude toward these things? Is it happiness, joy, and peace? Or is it stress, pain, and hurriedness? If you are similar to most, you will admit that your feelings are closer to the latter.

The truth is that most of us think of today as something—an obstacle, challenge, or necessary evil—to get through on the way toward a better day. We therefore rarely relish the present until it becomes another distant memory that we wish we could do over or relive. But even if we could jump ahead to a future day, it wouldn't be what we hope. That is because the future depends on the experiences of the present. That is, there are things we must go through today that shape the outcome of the future. We might as well enjoy the process.

Watch Out for These Present Stealers!

For too long we have contrasted enjoyment and godliness. Whether intended or not, it is often implied that holy living is serious and sober, while enjoyment is worldly and carnal. Consequently, for many the idea of enjoying life seems almost sinful.

I am not sure where this idea originated, but it didn't come from God. Jesus didn't die just to leave us miserable until we get to heaven. No, He revealed that one of the reasons He came to earth is for you and me to enjoy an abundant life here and now.

> The thief comes only to steal and kill and destroy. I came
> that they may have life, and have it abundantly.
>
> —JOHN 10:10

Certainly what Jesus says here shouldn't be mistaken for a life of mere fun and amusement or one in which everything is rosy. Rather, *life* here is the Greek word *zōē*, which is better defined as "a fully satisfied life that makes the most of every moment, regardless of the circumstances." It is a life that finds peace in the midst of chaos, remains positive through seasons of sorrow, and holds to hope when there seems no reason to. To be sure, it is not a life immune from difficulties but one that rises above the influence of them.

Are you ready to possess this abundant life that Jesus died to give? Do you truly want to *seize the day*? Later in the chapter, I will give some simple strategies to start. But first you must be alerted to some definite *present stealers*—some habits to avoid or stop. Let's explore several of these now.

Stop being too connected.

This might sound contradictory, but it is possible that an obsession with what is going on around you actually hinders you from enjoying your life.

Today, because of our ever-present connectivity through social media and mobile devices, we are almost obsessively in tune with what is happening in other people's lives. Log in to your favorite social network and what do you most often see? Pictures of smiling faces. Exciting adventures. Happy marriages. Major career advances. Everyone seems to be having the time of their lives. Everyone but you!

How does this make you feel? Depressed or anxious, most likely. The buzzword to describe this is *FOMO*, the fear of missing out.[2] Psychologists say that our constant connectedness creates a fear in people that they are missing out on something that everyone else is enjoying. This has at least a couple of negative effects. First, it causes comparison and keeps people under constant pressure to live like everyone else and to have what they have. Second, it feeds our digital addictions. We stay glued to our devices, stuck in an endless loop of refreshing our favorite social media accounts.

It is sad: we are often so engulfed in a world that doesn't exist that we disregard the people and events that are actually around us.

Stop being consumed by your ambitions.

"You are not doing enough!" Ever heard that nagging notion? I have. In fact, I admit that I am often at battle with a voice that blares, "You are not productive enough!" "You are not achieving enough!" and even "You are not accomplishing enough for God!"

Sure, drive is an admirable quality to possess. But as with anything, a good quality taken to extremes becomes a very dangerous quality. And those of us who are especially ambitious and driven toward goals have the tendency to get incredibly frustrated if we feel we are not making constant headway toward the mission.

The symptoms of this are often pathetic. I have made myself feel guilty for watching TV or lying down for a nap, regardless of what I achieved that day. I could have preached a sermon or authored an article that impacted thousands, but still a voice will nag, "You could be doing more."

Do you see how this steals your present? When you are so consumed with where you think you need to be, the simple joys and necessities of everyday life—relationships, fun, and rest— are viewed as distractions that don't contribute to where you are going. So you are made to feel guilty when you engage in them. That is no way to live!

Stop living for *when*.

Many people live on hold. That is, they living waiting for a certain situation or person to come along before they will allow themselves to be satisfied. It sounds similar to these statements:

- *When* I graduate, *then* I will have achieved something.
- *When* I get married, *then* I will be complete and happy.
- *When* I have children, *then* I will have a legacy worth living for.
- *When* I get to that level in my career, *then* I will have arrived.

If God has planted any of these desires in your heart, then absolutely pray and work toward them. But don't live for them.

By this I mean don't make them an idol. If education, marriage, children, a career, or any other life event is your benchmark for arriving, then you will possibly miss out on what God wants to teach or do through you in this season.

There are lots of joys to be experienced in this present moment. You can do things now that you can't do at other stages of life—when you have a spouse, children, or a higher-responsibility job. Don't waste this moment by wishing for another. The notion that you aren't happy or whole until you arrive at a certain situation only robs you of appreciating what God has given you today.

Stop being bitter or resentful.

I recall a particular time when I was hurt by someone who I felt consistently made disparaging comments about me. In hindsight I was likely oversensitive to some of it, but in the moment the remarks greatly offended me. Eventually I decided that I just didn't want to be around or hear about this person. This wasn't easy, however, because he and I were in a similar social circle with various friends in common. In short, I had to go to great lengths to avoid him or the mention of him!

I suppose that in some weird sort of way, I thought my avoidance would get him back for the things he said. But in truth he didn't even realize I was upset. All it did was make life much more complicated for me! Finally, more than a year later, the Lord spoke to me and said, "Kyle, I can't do the things you are asking me to do in your life if you continue to entangle yourself in this bitterness." Of course, the Lord was right. For the quality of my own life I needed to rid myself of this bitterness and seek forgiveness, which I did the next day.

The Bible speaks to this: "Watch out that no poisonous root of bitterness grows up to trouble you" (Heb. 12:15, NLT). Indeed, as I experienced, bitterness rarely affects someone else, but given enough attention, it will grow to give you trouble. Health studies support this truth. Bitterness, resentment, and unforgiveness can affect people physically with issues such as high blood pressure and heart disease.[3] At the least, these kill our quality of life by choking out any present happiness with anger, envy, and a bad attitude.

Simple Strategies to Start Enjoying Today

In chapter 6 I mentioned that scholars believe the Book of Psalms is intentionally arranged to tell the story of Israel's history with God. It is a fascinating study on its own. Each of the five books that make up the Psalms takes readers on the emotional journey of the nation coming to terms with God as their one, true King.

By books four and five (Psalms 90–150), there is a decided shift from the rest of the book. Largely the tone moves from lament and want to praise and thanksgiving. Notice in these final psalms that Israel makes a crucial decision that regardless of their situation they are going to praise God. Accordingly the remainder of Psalms is filled with sweeping faith declarations. One of my favorites is the determination to rejoice in the present day.

> This is the day that the LORD has made; let us rejoice and be glad in it.
> —PSALM 118:24

Understand that the declaration here isn't so much a reflection that their situation had suddenly changed. Rather, they changed their perspective about the situation. Their newfound decision to be thankful for the day was key to their present joy. And it is the same for you and me. You can't change every situation, but you can rise above the chaos and rejoice in whatever life brings. Here are some simple strategies that will help.

Start celebrating your progress.

After Solomon's temple was ravaged and the people scattered into foreign lands, Israel eventually had another opportunity to come together and to rebuild a second temple. They set out excitedly but got only as far as laying the foundation before opposition set in and the work stalled. With the project lingering in its infancy, the people became discouraged.

When it seemed the second temple would never get off the ground, God spoke into the situation and renewed His people's hope. Through the prophet Zechariah, He encouraged them not to be discouraged by a small beginning but to rejoice that the work was beginning (Zech. 4:10). In other words, God instructed Israel to celebrate the stage of the journey they were in—even if it was step one of one hundred.

I have had to take these words to heart many times. For years as I thought about the call of God to do what I am doing now— writing books, speaking, and using media for ministry—I became daunted by my grand visions but meager means. Still today, when the journey seems slow or overwhelming, God's words in Zechariah keep me going: "Don't despise these small beginnings, but rejoice that the work has begun."

God says the same to you. Celebrate your progress in whatever stage of the plan you find yourself. Certainly dream and prepare, but don't become frightened or discouraged by the road ahead. Step by step, day by day, the Lord will advance you toward what He has called you to do. Join God in His delight that the work has begun!

Give yourself permission to take a break!

This is a hard truth for a driven person like me to write. But it is a fact: God wants us to rest.

At the beginning of human history God instituted a law of rest known as a day of sabbath. He knew of the people's tendency to find identity in their work. This was especially true in the days before Jesus, when works were the basis of one's acceptance by God. But God ordained the Sabbath to force people to rest, which Jesus later revealed, "was made to meet the needs of people" (Mark. 2:27, NLT). In other words, God knows that we need to rest, so He established the Sabbath not so much as a law but as a lifesaver.

Certainly this doesn't mean that you should become a sluggard.

But this is permission to have completely unproductive moments and not feel guilty about them. Hear this: God says it is OK to take a break! Go to a ball game. Watch a decent movie. Enjoy a vacation. Set aside an evening to laugh with loved ones. You won't miss your destiny from a little downtime. Instead, you might just enrich it with memories to enjoy when you get there.

Start noticing the Holy Spirit in action.

A few years ago the Lord spoke to me about changing my somewhat cynical perspective of the world. He reminded me that His Holy Spirit is at work all the time, everywhere, and in every person. Therefore, rather than look at people and situations through the lens of "How is the devil working here?" I was challenged to discern, "How is the Holy Spirit working here?"

By focusing on the work of the Holy Spirit rather than the work of the devil, I began to value each moment as an opportunity for God's transformation in people and situations that I otherwise might have written off. This isn't always easy, and it definitely takes a retraining of the mind, but being tuned in to God's work helps to overcome the negativity of the 24/7 news cycle and remain positive through what is going on around you.

You can also use this perspective for how you view your own life. What struggles do you currently face? Know that God hasn't left you to deal with these by yourself. No, His Holy Spirit is at work in you even now, transforming you to be more like Jesus (2 Cor. 3:18). When you recognize the evidence of God's work in your life, you will begin to be excited about the day as one step closer to your breakthrough.

Start being content and thankful for what you have.

Paul gives perhaps the single greatest instruction to enjoy your life, which provides a great conclusion for this chapter: "Be content with what you have" (Heb. 13:5). This is absolutely crucial! You will never enjoy the present if you are envious of what someone else has or if you are chasing the dangling carrot of more and more and more.

I know that to some *contentment* seems like a bad word. Perhaps you think that to be content means to settle or even to give up. But that is not the meaning at all! To be content simply means that you have found a place of peaceful satisfaction with what you have and where you are in the moment. It means that you don't despise today and aren't desperate for tomorrow, but that you appreciate what God is doing right now.

Finally, to be content, you must count your blessings! Maybe that sounds cliché, but its truth is significant nonetheless. It is great to look ahead and believe God for a better situation, but as you dream, take a few moments to be thankful for the blessings God has given you. Living contentedly and thankfully helps you truly enjoy life and fully appreciate today for the gift it is.*

#ActivateTheWord
I enjoy my life.

The past is over, the future isn't here, and so I will fully live in the present moment that I am given. Whatever this day holds, I won't complain or be angry. I won't compare my life to anyone else's, but I am thankful for and content with the ways God has uniquely blessed me. This is the day the Lord has made; I will rejoice and be glad in it!

---

* Go Beyond the Book: Watch my short teaching titled "How to Get Off the Devil's Treadmill of Busyness" at www.kylewinkler.org/videos/how-to-get-off-the-devils -treadmill-of-busyness.

11

"THE JOY OF THE LORD IS MY STRENGTH"

*Do not be grieved, for the joy of
the LORD is your strength.*

—NEHEMIAH 8:10

I N ADDITION TO fear or worry, disappointment is one of the most common human emotions and a significant threat to enjoying our lives. The definition of *disappointment* is "the feeling of sadness or displeasure caused by the nonfulfillment of one's hopes or expectations."[1] As we all know, disappointment is a confusing and often very painful emotion. And given enough time, it can lead to long-term grief and strongholds of depression.

I have psyched myself up for plenty of events in my life that suddenly fell through at the last moment. I remember a TV interview that I had scheduled with a very popular evangelist. For months I ardently prepared for this opportunity that I believed would change the trajectory of my ministry. Then the day before we were set to film, the man's assistant called to let me know that he was sick and could no longer join me. Admittedly, I grieved over this for weeks!

Though my disappointment may seem small compared to what some have faced, this situation turned very serious because I didn't feel let down by the man but by God. I questioned why God would allow the man to get sick. Why would God have me

107

prepare for so long just to steal the opportunity away so quickly? Even worse, I was tempted to question God's goodness. Being disappointed by God is the most dangerous place to be, yet so many of us have been there or perhaps are in that place right now.

So what do you do in moments such as these, when life doesn't go as you hoped or planned? How do you overcome the grief after you gave it your all but you didn't make the team or the cast, get into the school, or get the job? The spouse you expected to grow old with has fallen out of love with you? The baby you dreamed of and carried didn't make it to birth? The prophetic word you sincerely believed was from God turned out very differently?

I could mention myriad other circumstances. Nonetheless, as we will see, the answer to these questions can be found in the stories and realizations of many throughout the Bible who struggled through similar situations.

Israel's Journey to True Satisfaction

Perhaps nobody knows more about dealing with disappointment and discouragement than the Israelites. Consider the ups and downs of their story. Through miraculous means God rescued His people from captivity in Egypt with the grandiose promise that they would arrive in "their own fertile and spacious land... flowing with milk and honey" (Exod. 3:8, NLT). This Promised Land He later assured would be a place where they would enjoy rest from their enemies and have a temple in which to worship Him (2 Sam. 7:10–12).

After it seemed as if everything was going as planned, all was stolen away—the temple was destroyed and many of the people were deported by their enemies into foreign lands. Understandably the people were deeply grieved and left wondering, "What happened to God's promise?"

Israel spent decades in exile but eventually was allowed to return home to Jerusalem. Imagine their emotions as they reentered their once beautiful city in ruins. Nonetheless, they quickly went to work to rebuild what they once had—a temple for worship and a wall for protection. Still, the restoration of these things didn't bring the satisfaction they expected, and the people felt great distress.

In their time of pain and sorrow Israel made a crucial decision that changed everything. They decided to look to God's Word for help. It must have been a beautiful sight. After a public reading of God's Word, thousands of once wayward Israelites lifted their hands, bowed their heads, and worshipped (Neh. 8:6). As they praised through their grief, the leaders made a transformational declaration over the people: "Do not be grieved, for the joy of the LORD is your strength" (Neh. 8:10). What a powerful proclamation for weary people who had been through so much! After this, the Bible records that the people went away with great joy because "they had understood the words that were declared to them" (Neh. 8:12).

What exactly did the people understand that filled them with such joy? After everything they had been through, I believe they came to two profound revelations that I want to explore now.

Happiness does not equal satisfaction.

The notion of happiness is a North Star that guides many of us. Think about its power. We enter into a relationship because it makes us feel happy. Most of our ambitions are driven by the idea that accomplishing a certain goal will make us happy. And the moment we realize that any of these don't bring us what we expected, we move on to something else that might do it.

So what is this force that has the world under its spell? *Happiness* is defined as "a feeling or showing of pleasure." [2] It is an emotion of euphoria, excitement, or bliss. Scientists have performed extensive studies on the feeling and have discovered it to be determined by various things. They found that 50 percent of happiness is determined by genetics, 40 percent by daily activities, and 10 percent by circumstances. [3]

The study reveals why people are on a never-ending pursuit of happiness: if it is determined by genetics, it can't be controlled; if it is determined by daily activities, it is not lasting; if it is determined by circumstances, it comes and goes. Happiness, like any other feeling or emotion, is temporal and temperamental. One day we feel it; the next day we don't.

Understand that I don't mean to associate happiness with evil. God created emotions and feelings to enrich our lives. But problems quickly arise when these get out of balance. God never intended for us to make decisions based on feelings or emotions, and happiness is no exception. For our own good He doesn't want us to chase after or be led by something that is here today and gone tomorrow.

Pursuing happiness is the trap the Israelites fell into, which led to their great distress. From the very beginning they misinterpreted God's promises with the expectation that everything would feel good. Thus, when they encountered the inevitable struggles of life, they were let down, became depressed, and sought other often sinful ways to experience pleasure.

We must be careful that we don't fall into the same trap. When we set happiness to be the goal of life, we set ourselves up for disappointment. People, possessions, and life circumstances were never meant to be the source of our satisfaction. Your spouse was never intended to make you feel good all the time. Your work was never intended to be the source of your security. Your house, car, boat, and bank account were never meant to be the measuring stick of your success. Don't place your well-being in something that is ever changing. Just as Israel was, you will only be let down and left wondering, "What happened?"

The source of satisfaction is trust in the Lord.

The public reading of God's Word by Israel was a pivotal moment when they refocused on God Himself—His goodness, faithfulness, and everlasting love—rather than on what they expected He would give them. And the result was that this new focus gave them much more than a happy feeling—it gave them true *joy*.

To continue what we explored in the previous chapter, the

final two books in Psalms (Psalms 90–150) reveal the drastic shift in the Israelites' understanding. We see in these chapters some amazing acknowledgments about who God is:

- "Lord, you have been our dwelling place in all generations" (Ps. 90:1).
- "Because you have made the LORD your refuge... no evil shall befall you" (Ps. 91:9–10).
- "The LORD is king, he is robed in majesty" (Ps. 93:1).

Here we read that God's people had finally arrived at the place where He had always wanted them. They found that their contentment wasn't in a piece of land, but in the Lord as their dwelling place. Their security wasn't in horses, chariots, or a wall, but in the Lord. The well-being of the nation wasn't in a human king, but in the Lord as their one, true King.

In the Lord, God's people finally found something much greater than mere emotion, a feeling of pleasure, or even an expected blessing. In the Lord, Israel found a constant and steady state of gladness, peace, and contentment. Yes, when they finally refocused their source of delight from temporal circumstances to trusting God's unchanging qualities and the faithfulness of His Word, then they found a satisfaction worth celebrating—they found true joy!

How to Cultivate the Joy of the Lord

Like Israel, many of our favorite New Testament heroes also found the joy of the Lord to be their source of strength through great trials and persecution. In fact, the apostle Paul considered joy to be a hallmark of the Christian life, so much so that he listed it as a fruit of God's Spirit within us.

> The fruit of the Spirit is love, *joy*, peace, patience, kindness, generosity, faithfulness, gentleness, and self-control.
> —GALATIANS 5:22–23

Here and all throughout the New Testament the Greek word for *joy* is *chara*. This word is related to *charisma*, which means "grace" and is often used by Paul to describe the spiritual gifts given by God (1 Cor. 12:4–10). Here again, this passage reveals that joy is not a feeling we derive from external circumstances but is a gift from God that is planted within each of us at the moment of salvation.

What this means is that you already have joy in you. You don't have to pray, "Lord, give me joy!" Rather, like any fruit, there are things you can do to cultivate, grow, and strengthen joy. Let's look at some New Testament situations for practical lessons on how to do this in our lives today.

Focus on the truth that God believes in you.

Nearly anytime the early apostles made progress, some sort of trial set them back. The Book of Acts details an account of when they performed many signs and wonders, and therefore new believers were added to the church in droves. But immediately after this exhilarating experience religious leaders became jealous and imprisoned them.

Persecution, however, is no match for God's might. During the night an angel of the Lord opened the prison doors and charged the men to go to the temple and preach (Acts 5:20). When the apostles did as they were told, they were then ordered to appear before a council where they faced a death sentence but were instead severely beaten and then let go!

Through this roller coaster of emotions—miracles to imprisonment to deliverance to near death to release—the apostles weren't phased. The Bible says, rather, that as they left, they *rejoiced* and kept on with even greater audacity (Acts 5:41–42).

How could the apostles cultivate joy in times that surely felt unpredictable, discouraging, and downright scary? They saw themselves worthy to suffer disgrace for the name of Jesus (Acts 5:41). In other words, they could joyfully face any trial because they saw themselves handpicked by God as ones who could handle the persecution.

Similarly you will find joy and strength by focusing on God's optimistic belief in you. The Bible assures that God will not let you be tempted or tried beyond your strength (1 Cor. 10:13). When you are faced with a challenge you feel is insurmountable, find joy in the fact that God believes in you so much that He thinks you can take it. God believes you can handle this day. You can handle this relationship. You can handle this task or job. Rejoice! God believes you will endure—you will overcome!

Praise God, especially when you don't feel like it.

On the way to a place of prayer, Paul and his companion Silas were confronted by a girl with a spirit of divination. Annoyed by her spastic outbursts, Paul finally ordered the spirit to come out of her, which it did. The townsfolk, however, weren't too happy with the girl's deliverance because the evil spirit within her made them a lot of money in the fortune-telling business. And so, for the crime of disturbing the local economy, Paul and Silas found themselves severely beaten and thrown in prison (Acts 16:16–24.)

This conflict marked Paul's first time in prison for his faith. Regardless of the miracles he previously experienced, I am sure he felt fear and even questioned God's plan in all of it. Still, Paul didn't allow his doubts and feelings to plunge him into disappointment, depression, or hopelessness. No, he and Silas doubled down against their feelings by praising! At about midnight—when their bodies were surely exhausted—the two cultivated joy by praying and singing hymns to God. Then miraculously, an earthquake broke open the doors and unfastened the chains of everyone in the prison (Acts 16:25–34)!

Praise is powerful! But like Paul and Silas, to be most effective, you can't wait until your situation changes and you feel like praising. No, real joy arises when you praise in faith because of who God is. When you begin to praise in the midst of sadness, grief, loneliness, or pain, your entire countenance changes because your mind shifts from being focused on your situation to being focused on the power of your awesome God.

Replace negative thoughts with God's promises.

Paul wrote to the church at Philippi: "Rejoice in the Lord always; again I will say, Rejoice" (Phil. 4:4). The fact that Paul could say such a thing in this place was amazing. Philippi was the city where he and Silas were imprisoned for casting out the spirit of divination. And Paul later described it as a place where they had "suffered and been shamefully mistreated" (1 Thess. 2:2).

Astonishingly, even in the place of some of his greatest hardships, Paul encouraged the people to rejoice and not to worry (Phil. 4:6). The method by which he instructed that this is possible is one of the most important principles for cultivating joy in our lives today. Paul wrote:

> Finally, beloved, whatever is true, whatever is honorable, whatever is just, whatever is pure, whatever is pleasing, whatever is commendable, if there is any excellence and if there is anything worthy of praise, think about these things.
> —PHILIPPIANS 4:8

In essence, Paul instructs that the secret to joy is to replace negative thoughts with positive ones.

The most effective way that I have found to replace my negative thoughts is to do what we are learning throughout this book. What is more true, honorable, pure, and worthy of praise than the truth of God's Word? Nothing! So replace your thoughts with God's Word. When you are overwhelmed, find strength in the declaration: "In my weariness, I come to Jesus and He gives me rest" (Matt. 11:28–30). Nervous? Proclaim, "God keeps me in perfect peace" (Isa. 26:3). Depressed? Confess, "I live refreshed and full of joy because God is my comfort and encouragement" (2 Cor.

7:6). Yes, as God's Word assures, when your mind is steadfast on the goodness of God, you will be kept in perfect peace (Isa. 26:3).

It Is Time to Shift Your Focus

Let's return now to the question I asked at the beginning of this chapter. What do you do when life doesn't go as planned or God's promises don't work out as you thought? The answer that is revealed all throughout the Bible is that you should dig deeper, trust harder, and praise more!

Disappointing moments aren't times to look elsewhere or away from the Lord, but these are moments to stare more deeply into who He is. I know that sounds contradictory. But when you are grieving from letdowns by people or circumstances, or even when it feels as if God Himself let you down, the only lasting solution to renewed strength and hope is to look beyond the surface of how things appear or how they feel. Instead, you must press in all the more to the truths of God's Word—that He is good, His ways are higher, and He is in control. When you shift your focus from an ever-changing feeling or situation to your never-changing God, you will experience a strength, peace, and satisfaction that endure the tests of time.*

#ActivateTheWord
The joy of the Lord is my strength!

I don't look to people, possessions, or circumstances for my satisfaction. Instead, I find my well-being in God. I will not be grieved by letdowns! My encouragement and strength are built on the truth that God is good, He is faithful, and He is in control.

---

* Go Beyond the Book: Watch my short teaching titled "Why God Doesn't Want You to Be Happy" at www.kylewinkler.org/videos/why-god-doesnt-want-you-to-be-happy.

12

"SOMETHING GOOD WILL HAPPEN TO ME"

I believe that I shall see the goodness of the LORD in the land of the living.

—PSALM 27:13

GOD IS A law-giving, law-abiding God. As we learned in chapter 1, He created the universe to be governed by a host of physical laws such as gravity, centrifugal force, and inertia. These laws are constant and unchanging and give us faith that what worked yesterday will work the same today and tomorrow.

We also learned that woven into the very foundations of creation are supernatural and spiritual laws. Some of these described in Scripture include the following:

- The law of God's Word to sustain and uphold all things (Heb. 1:3).

- The law of sin to destroy all things (Rom. 6:23).

- The law of the harvest that you later reap from what you earlier sowed (Gal. 6:7).

Like the physical laws, these spiritual laws are largely unseen and their effects are equally as evident.

The Law of Expectation

A powerful, supernatural law that I want to explore in this chapter is one that is part and parcel to the law of God's spoken Word. In fact, it is a key element in activating the power of God's Word. It is what I call the law of expectation.

Essentially, the law of expectation means that you eventually get what you expect. This can be either negative or positive. If you expect to have a bad day, you will have a bad day. If you expect the favor of God, you will receive the favor of God. If you expect a breakthrough, you will eventually experience a breakthrough. And so on. To be sure, this isn't just my opinion; you can trace the law of expectation all throughout Scripture.

David expected God's goodness in the midst of trouble.

King David offers some of my favorite illustrations regarding the power of expectation. In the midst of extremely tenuous circumstances, the psalms of David reveal a profound faith that was the key to his confidence, courage, and success.

Psalm 27 is a perfect example of this. To provide context, scholars believe that David wrote this psalm while he was in the midst of great trouble, possibly even the death of his parents.[1] Whatever the situation, the psalm certainly portrays moments of intense distress.

As armies encamped around him and accusers spoke lies about him, David made a declaration of expectation. "I believe that I shall see the goodness of the LORD in the land of the living," he exclaimed (Ps. 27:13). What David meant by this is that he sincerely believed that God would deliver him—not at a future time or in a future place, but right here and right now.

Deliverance is precisely what David experienced. In fact, 2 Samuel 8 asserts that "while David was king of Israel, he won many battles" (v. 1, NIRV). Time and time again, God honored David's declaration by giving him just what he expected—God's goodness in the midst of trouble.

A woman expected instant relief from her infirmity.

The Gospels recount the story of a woman whose expectation was said to instantly heal her. At the time when Jesus was attracting great crowds because of His miracles, a woman who suffered from hemorrhaging pressed through to get close to Jesus. In twelve years of suffering the woman had expended all her money on physicians and was growing worse by the day. But the woman heard about the healing power of Jesus, and every ounce of hope she had left she placed in Him.

The woman's words as she pushed through the crowd to touch Jesus reveal her expectation: "If I but touch his clothes, I will be made well" (Mark 5:28). Upon her confident assertion, the Bible records that the hemorrhaging stopped and the woman was immediately healed. After Jesus had realized what happened, He encouraged the woman, assuring her, "Daughter, your faith has made you well" (Mark 5:34). In other words, Jesus said that her audacious expectation was the basis of her healing.

Paul overcame the worst with expectations of the best.

The Bible includes illustrations about how people overcome the worst with expectations of the best. In Acts, Paul details a shipwreck that took place during his journey to Rome. At one point in the excursion, the fury of a storm hit them so hard that his shipmates began to throw their cargo and fishing tackle overboard. After days of being tossed around by the winds and rain, the crew was convinced that they wouldn't make it to land alive. In fact, in this moment they expressed a negative expectation: "All hope of our being saved was at last abandoned" (Acts 27:18–20).

The crew's expectation of the worst came because they set their eyes on the situation at hand and lost sight of the goal. But Paul righted the ship, so to speak. He spoke up in an attempt to change their expectations and thus change their fate. "I urge you now to keep up your courage, for there will be no loss of life among you, but only of the ship," Paul encouraged (Acts 27:22). Indeed, Paul's expectations were met. Though the ship was lost, every person on board was saved.

The Foundations of Our Expectation

Certainly there must be a valid reason for whatever you expect. That is, you must have a real, biblical basis for your confidence. Let's look a bit more closely at the few illustrations we just reviewed in order to derive the three primary foundations of positive expectations.

Character of God

David had such an intimate relationship with the Lord that he knew God is faithful and loving and desires good things for His people. And thus David made a declaration based on God's character. Today, not only do we have the benefit of knowing the character of God through the 24/7 presence of His Holy Spirit in our lives, but we also have God's Word that reveals who He is and what He wants.

One of my favorite truths that helps me build great expectations is that God desires to "accomplish abundantly far more than all we can ask or imagine" (Eph. 3:20). The thought of this is incomprehensible. What are you dreaming of and praying about right now? Base your expectation about its outcome on the truth of God's character: He wants to do something infinitely beyond what you could ever hope.

The history of God

The woman with the issue of blood built her confidence that she would be healed based on stories of others who were healed before her. This is a very effective way to build faith and expectation that is modeled even in modern church history.

Consider some of the great moves of God within the twentieth century, all of which were coupled with tremendous miracles. The Azusa Street revival of 1906, for example, quickly spread from a church in California to churches on other continents, simply by the sharing of stories. When people around the world heard about the miracles in their meetings, their faith was built to expect that what God was doing for others, He could also do for them. And indeed, God honored these expectations. Through this, many millions experienced His power, which later contributed to the rise of the Pentecostal and Charismatic movements we know of today.

If you need an instant boost of confidence that God will work something out in your life, begin to study the stories of God's power in the lives of others. Read about people who were healed or delivered or who received miraculous provision. Remember, God doesn't show favoritism (Rom. 2:11). If He did it for someone else, He can also do it for you!

The Word of God

Finally, Paul's confidence that he and his crew would make it out alive came because He set his eyes on God's Word. The Lord had revealed to Him that he would stand before the emperor, and thus Paul determined to trust God's Word over even a seemingly deadly storm (Acts 27:23–24).

Paul's expectation founded on the assurance of God's Word is an extremely practical method for us today. With thousands of promises throughout Scripture, some of which we are exploring throughout this book, we have plenty of reasons for great expectations.

Expectation Demands Action

Whatever you expect, whether healing, financial breakthrough, the salvation of a loved one, or something else, know that expectations don't become reality by merely wishing, believing, or hoping. No, the law of expectation works because proper expectation puts actions to hopes. This is what James instructed:

> So faith by itself, if it has no works, is dead.
>
> —JAMES 2:17

In other words, James said that faith, though crucial, doesn't accomplish much on its own, but to be effective, faith needs to be coupled with action. That is, there is a part that you must do, and then there is a part that only God can do. Let's now explore two key ways to bring your expectations to life.

Pray in faith.

The majority of our prayers sound similar to this: "Lord, please give me a job so that I can afford to provide for my family"; "God, I really desire a wife; please send one my way"; or "Jesus, please take this problem away from me." If we spoke to other people the way we often speak to God, people would accuse us of begging all the time!

Thankfully God doesn't accuse us of anything; He is happy that we talk to Him. But God doesn't want us to be *beggars*, pleading with Him to "give me, give me, give me." No, God desires for us to be *believers* who are assured that He hears our prayers and because of His goodness wants to give us good gifts. This is what Jesus taught us about prayer.

> Whatever you ask for in prayer with faith, you will receive.
> —MATTHEW 21:22

James wrote something similar. Regarding how to pray, he instructed, "Ask in faith, never doubting" (James 1:6).

The Bible teaches that God desires us to pray with the expectation that He will give us the answer or solution for which we are praying. This means that rather than pray a beggar's prayer— "Lord, please give me this job"—we should pray a believer's prayer—"Lord, I thank you that you desire to provide for me, and I trust that you will bring me the perfect job to help meet my needs." Do you see the difference in these two prayers? The first contains an element of doubt, but the second is built on what we believe about God and His goodness.

The most common question about praying in faith is "How

can we be entirely sure that what we are praying is in accordance with God's will?" I appreciate how Jerry Bridges tackles this:

> The object of our faith is God Himself; not our faith. When I do not have faith, I'm saying…either God cannot answer this prayer or God will not answer this prayer. If I say He cannot, I'm questioning His sovereignty and His power. If I say He will not, I'm questioning His goodness. To pray in faith means that I believe God can and I believe God will insofar as it is consistent with His glory, because God is good.[2]

Finally, in addition to praying according to what we know about God's character, we may pray bold, expectant prayers because we know the will of God as it is written in Scripture. For example, as we will learn in chapter 15, God promises to supply all our needs (Phil. 4:19). And so, when praying for provision, we should thank God for it, even if we don't yet see it. In fact, we should pray this way about all God's promises. God appreciates when we believe in Him, His goodness, and His Word so much that we should pray with absolute certainty that He will make good on His promises.

Speak in faith.

Evangelist Oral Roberts led more than three hundred healing crusades around the world, at which his ministry estimates he laid hands on more than two million people. His legacy will be forever remembered by dramatic miracles but also for an infamous declaration that reveals much about the source of these miracles: "Something good is going to happen to you today!"

Roberts's ministry was so successful in part because he employed the practice of speaking in faith. This means that he made a declaration of expectation about something that he hadn't yet seen. Though Roberts couldn't be assured of the outcome in the natural, he could declare that something good was going to happen because He knew that this belief was consistent with God's character and God's Word. So Roberts wasn't speaking out his own magic words; he was standing on God's Word by doing what Jesus instructed:

> If you do not doubt in your heart, *but believe that what you say will come to pass*, it will be done for you.
>
> —MARK 11:23

Finally, while it is important to speak God's Word in faith in prayer or in spiritual warfare, it is equally as important to speak in faith during regular conversations with people.

Consider your lunchroom or watercooler talk. How much of it consists of lifeless words founded in complaints, worry, or bitterness? Have you ever murmured something such as, "This job is going to kill me"? I have! And while it seems innocent enough, speaking in this way keeps your mind focused on defeat and certainly doesn't take into account God's grace or His joy as your strength.

It is fine to acknowledge the reality of your circumstances, but I challenge you to couple it with expectation. Here's an example: "This job is tough, this boss is difficult to work for, but I believe God will give me strength. I trust that He will show me His goodness." Speaking this way definitely goes against the grain of our flesh, and it takes much practice and intention. But speaking in faith even during casual conversation keeps your mind focused on God's goodness, which keeps you refreshed and makes it more enjoyable for others to be in your presence.

Change Your Expectations, Change Your Life

Your expectations influence your behaviors, which ultimately change your life. I experienced the power of this through a physical issue that I dealt with just before writing this book.

For more than a year I suffered from inflammation in my rotator cuff, which caused great pain during certain motions. Because of the pain I eventually began to change my movements and posture to avoid discomfort. I changed the way I put on shirts and jackets and even how I got out of bed in the morning. The problem with this was that my body adapted to the pain in an unnatural way, which triggered other muscles to overcompensate. So in addition to dealing with a tender shoulder, I also suffered with the symptoms of a stiff neck!

Finally, I went to the doctor to have it checked out, and he prescribed physical therapy. After months of rotator-cuff-strengthening exercises, the shoulder issue finally resolved. However, though I was healed, I still dealt with the other symptoms. And here is where I learned a great lesson about the power of expectation and how it affects life. Because I lived with the pain for so long, I simply expected it to be there. Therefore, well after I was healed, these expectations caused my body to anticipate the pain, which caused the other issues to persist. To experience full healing, I had to overcome this expectation of pain and intentionally change my mind according to the truth that I was healed. When I changed my thinking, my behaviors began to change, and the other issues eventually went away.

What expectations do you need to change? Just because you were once a victim doesn't mean you will always be a victim. Just because you were once rejected doesn't mean you will always be rejected. Perhaps you have suffered through years of pain or disappointment, but you don't have to continue to expect to experience the same today or tomorrow. No, you can overcome any of the effects of negative expectations by praying, thinking, and speaking according to the truth of God's Word. As I learned, when you begin to change your expectations, you will begin to change your life.*

---

* Go Beyond the Book: Watch my short teaching titled "Overcoming Expectations of Pain" at www.kylewinkler.org/videos/overcoming-expectations-of-pain.

#ActivateTheWord
Something good will happen to me!

I know that God is great and desires the best for me. And so I trust that any pain, sorrow, or struggle is being used by God to bring about His goodness in my life. Because God's power is working in me to accomplish far more than I can ever ask or imagine, I pray, think, speak, and live with great expectations.

PART FOUR

STRATEGIC DECLARATIONS TO OVERCOME OBSTACLES

13

"I CAN DO WHATEVER GOD WANTS ME TO DO"

I can do all things through him who strengthens me.

—PHILIPPIANS 4:13

HAVE YOU EVER felt the fear and unease of being way beyond your own ability? What about the insecurity of feeling that you don't have what it takes to accomplish a certain responsibility? I have! About halfway through writing my first book, I remember suddenly being confronted with the dread that I was in over my head with the whole process. For a few weeks, I was daunted by how much was left to write, the deadline that was looming, and the little that I felt I had left to say. With this, my mind shifted from the excitement of the opportunity to fears of failure. Numerous mornings I would awaken with nagging anxiety that I just couldn't complete the manuscript.

At the height of it all, when I was tired, my mind felt spent, the words just wouldn't come together, and time was ticking, I raised my hands in protest. "I can't do this!" I shouted to the Lord. "I have come to the end of myself."

What I didn't realize at the time is that this declaration was the catalyst for my turnaround. You see, coming to the end of myself was exactly the place the Lord wanted me to get to in this process. Coming to the end of myself meant that I was beyond my own thoughts, words, abilities, and strengths. It meant that I was no longer in control but was solely dependent on God's Spirit.

Within minutes of my protest—or maybe it was my surrender—I received an illustration that helped me complete a section of the book that I was stressing over. From that day forward I began my writing routine with the declaration, "OK, God, it is just You and me, and I want a whole lot more of You than me!" Of course, God was always faithful! Whenever anxiety attempted to rear its ugly head again, confessing these words of surrender brought me a supernatural peace that helped me finish the manuscript and see all other simultaneous responsibilities through to completion. Truly, when I came to the end of myself, God's Spirit took over and empowered me to do just what I needed to do.

Do you feel weak or weary about something you face right now? Are you up against a deadline or a seemingly impossible responsibility? Does it appear as if you have been thrown into the deep end before learning how to swim? Then you have arrived at a great place! You have arrived at an opportunity to truly surrender to the Lord and to let His power do what you never thought possible.

The Source of Our Power

In over their heads is the position the apostles likely felt they were in upon the ascension of Jesus back to heaven. Just imagine their insecurity. Jesus commissioned them to "go into all the world and proclaim the good news to the whole creation" (Mark 16:15). But with Jesus gone, how could they do this? Their history of doing things outside His presence was pitiful, after all. They were crippled by fear in a boat as a storm raged (Matt 14:22–26). They failed to cast out a demon from a mute boy (Mark 9:14–29). They fell asleep as Jesus went away to pray in the garden (Luke 22:39–46). When questioned by authorities, the most loyal even refused to acknowledge his relationship with his beloved Messiah (John 18:15–18). Yes, their lousy track record when away from Jesus likely gave them plenty of reason to worry that they couldn't possibly fulfill Jesus's Great Commission on their own. The task was just too monumental!

But Jesus never intended for the apostles to accomplish the goal on their own. No, just before His ascension Jesus freshly reminded His followers of the promise He spoke of so frequently—the gift of God's Holy Spirit, who would come to enable His followers to do what they could never do on their own. "Wait here for the promise," Jesus instructed. "You will be baptized with the Holy Spirit.... You will receive power...and you will be my witnesses in Jerusalem, in all Judea and Samaria, and to the ends of the earth" (Acts 1:5, 8).

Do you recall the rest of the story? Immediately upon His ascension, the apostles and some 120 believers gathered to wait for the promise of this power, though they weren't quite sure what it would look like. Within days the power came. With wind, fire, and frenzy, God's Holy Spirit swept through the room and filled all who were in attendance with a power they never had outside of the physical presence of Jesus. (See Acts 2.)

The firstfruit of this newfound power in their lives is seen in Peter's reaction. This man, who just days before was too fearful to acknowledge that he even knew Jesus, suddenly stood up and more than acknowledged Him—He preached a bold sermon to multitudes in attendance. As a result about three thousand people were added to the faith in a single day (Acts 2:41).

Peter's unnatural boldness and ability became the common evidence of the Holy Spirit in the lives of all who believed. The Book of Acts chronicles the Spirit's arrival through four more instances after the Day of Pentecost: on the Samaritans (Acts 8), on Paul (Acts 9), on the Gentiles (Acts 10), and on the Ephesians (Acts 19). While I don't have the space here to review each of these in depth, after study you will notice that the primary experience of those filled with God's Holy Spirit was the empowerment to do something that they couldn't otherwise do on their own.

Jesus Calls You to Impossible Tasks Too

The power of the Holy Spirit to do the impossible wasn't just relegated to select groups within the early church. No, Jesus promised the Spirit as an advocate who would be with all God's people forever (John 14:16). Likewise, Peter proclaimed that the Holy Spirit was God's gift for "everyone whom the Lord our God calls to him" (Acts 2:39). And in Acts, Luke provided us with a clue that we should pursue and expect the same power that empowered the early church. Allow me to explain.

Acts begins with Christ's commission to reach "the ends of the earth" (Acts 1:8). The remainder of the book chronicles this mission, made possible by His power, through Jerusalem, Judea, and Samaria. But the book closes with Paul imprisoned in Rome, obviously short of the ends of the earth. Surely Luke knew the rest of the story, so why didn't he share it?

Many scholars believe the answer lies in a literary technique used in those days, which leaves off the ending so that the reader will continue the story in his or her life.[1] The significance of this is monumental! It means Luke intended to convey that you and I are to continue the works of Jesus through the same supernatural power of the Holy Spirit.

Indeed, just as Jesus called those in the early church, He calls us to impossible tasks, including far greater things than even He saw in His own ministry. Just before He revealed the coming of His Holy Spirit to His disciples, He promised this: "Very truly, I tell you, the one who believes in me will also do the works that I do and, in fact, will do greater works than these, because I am going to the Father" (John 14:12).

Perhaps it is curious to you how Jesus's return back to the Father enables you and me to do greater works. Wouldn't we be more powerful if Jesus were still on earth today? Surprisingly, no. While on earth Jesus was not omnipresent. That is, He was limited to a single human body that could be in only one place at one time. Because He returned to the Father, however, He released His Holy Spirit, who He promised would be present in every believer everywhere and at all times.

Think about some of the works Jesus did during His short ministry on earth. He healed the sick, cast out demons, resisted temptation by the devil, preached to multitudes, endured persecution, showed great compassion to the hurting, and even overcame the power of death. Amazingly, He didn't accomplish any of this out of His own strength of being God in the flesh. No, He did it in the way that He assured we too can do the same and greater works—by the empowerment of the Holy Spirit.

> The Spirit of God, who raised Jesus from the dead, lives in you.
> And just as God raised Christ Jesus from the dead, he will give
> life to your mortal bodies by this same Spirit living within you.
> —ROMANS 8:11, NLT

The magnitude of this truth is unfathomable. While on earth Jesus "gave up his divine privileges" and depended solely on the empowerment of the Holy Spirit (Phil. 2:7, NLT). In doing so, He modeled how we too can be obedient to everything God asks of us. To do the impossible, you don't have to be God; you just have to let Him in and let Him take control.

You Can Do Whatever You Need to Do

The New Testament gives many names for the Holy Spirit, often determined by the particular role being described. These include "the promise of the Father" (Acts 1:4), "Helper" (John 14:26, ESV), and "Advocate" (John 14:16), among others. Paul, however, often chose to refer to the Holy Spirit as the "Spirit of Christ" or the "Spirit of [God's] Son" (Rom. 8:9; Gal. 4:6).

In relating the Spirit as Christ, Paul emphasized that the power of Jesus we just reviewed lives inside of each believer. In fact, it was the presence of the Spirit of Christ through whom Paul boasted that he could do all things:

> I can do all things through him who strengthens me.
> —Philippians 4:13

"I can do all things through Christ…" is one of the most beloved declarations of the faith. We see it on posters and wall art, on bracelets and greeting cards, and even painted on the faces of sports personalities. At first glance, Paul's words seem to bolster our American idea of personal empowerment—that we can achieve whatever we set our minds to. People use these words to build self-esteem in their potential to acquire great wealth, ace tests, lose weight, win games, or get jobs.

While it might be very inspirational to apply Philippians 4:13 to whatever we desire, the context in which Paul actually declared it gives it a somewhat different meaning. The preceding verses make Paul's intent very clear:

> Not that I am referring to being in need; for I have learned
> to be content with whatever I have. I know what it is to
> have little, and I know what it is to have plenty. In any and
> all circumstances I have learned the secret of being well-fed
> and of going hungry, of having plenty and of being in need.
> —Philippians 4:11–12

It is after saying all this that Paul then asserts, "I can do all things through him who strengthens me." Understand that Paul's words weren't those of self-empowerment, turning him into a superman who was able to bust out of the prison from which he wrote this passage. Rather, Christ's Spirit in Paul empowered him to endure the difficulties and challenges of his calling. He was strengthened to achieve exactly what God had ordained him to achieve. And most importantly, he was able to go through it all with the joy of contentment and the assurance that God would finish what He started.

What Paul's declaration means to you is that the Holy Spirit will supernaturally empower you to do whatever God asks you to do.

- If God calls you into ministry, He will provide the funds and the opportunities.

- If God asks you to stay in a difficult job, situation, or relationship, He will provide the grace to stick it out with a hopeful attitude.

- If God asks you to give beyond your means, He will provide the finances to meet your needs.

- If you are raising a child by yourself, God will provide the physical and emotional support you need to do it successfully.

- If you are in a crisis or a challenging circumstance, God will provide the wisdom to help you navigate through it.

What is it you have to do? Know that whatever it is, God never planned for you to do it on your own. No, He will do the heavy lifting if you will do the heavy trusting.

How to Let Go and Let God Take Over

As I learned during some of the daunting moments of my ministry, the same Holy Spirit who raised Jesus from the dead, empowered the early church to fulfill Christ's commission, and kept Paul content in his calling will undoubtedly strengthen you to do what you never thought you could. Here is how to put this all into practice so you can let go and let God take over.

Step 1: Surrender striving.

There is no other choice: you must give up trying to make everything happen on your own. Your strength is a limited resource; it runs out. So rip off your Superman or Wonder Woman cape! You were not created to be all things to all people, nor to do all things on your own. No, you were created to be dependent on God's Spirit, who is an unlimited source of power. The first step of supernatural strength is to lift your hands in surrender, as I did, and admit, "God, I can't do this on my own! I need your strength." Now immediately proceed to step 2.

Step 2: Ask to be freshly filled with the Holy Spirit.

Though the Holy Spirit enters you at the moment of your salvation, subsequently you can be filled and saturated with the Spirit's power on a continual basis. In fact, the Bible models this as the source of the disciples' ongoing strength.

> And the disciples were continually filled with joy and with the Holy Spirit.
>
> —ACTS 13:52, NASB

As the disciples did, you and I should seek the *ongoing*, fresh infilling of God's Spirit to strengthen us. To do this, I encourage you to awaken each morning with a simple prayer: "Father, I ask for a fresh filling of Your Holy Spirit. Saturate me with Your presence. Fill me with Your power. Strengthen me to do what I need to do today." The Bible assures that God gives His Spirit to anyone who asks (Luke 11:13). So after praying this, be confident that you are immediately filled afresh with the Holy Spirit.

Step 3: Wait in expectation for God's power to manifest.

At His ascension Jesus instructed His disciples to wait for the power of the Holy Spirit, who would come to enable them to fulfill Christ's commission. Still, as we learned, they had no idea when this would happen or what this would look like. So they had to wait with expectation and trust.

In just a matter of days the apostles received just what Jesus promised—a supernatural strength not of themselves, to do what they could never do on their own. The prophet Isaiah spoke of this same principle many years before:

> But those who wait for the LORD shall renew their strength,
> they shall mount up with wings like eagles, they shall run
> and not be weary, they shall walk and not faint.
>
> —ISAIAH 40:31

What a promise! God doesn't say you *might* find new strength; He promises you *will!* Like the disciples, all you have to do is wait in expectation of it. Be assured: real breakthrough happens when you stop depending on what you can do and start trusting in what God will do in spite of you.*

#ActivateTheWord
I can do whatever God wants me to do!

Because the Spirit of Christ is in me, I am filled with the same power that raised Jesus from the dead and am empowered to do the greater works He promised. Christ in me gives me strength when I am weak, clarity when I feel confused, the right words when I need them, hope when I feel discouraged, joy when I am weary, and the ability to do whatever God asks of me.

---

* Go Beyond the Book: Watch my short teaching titled "The Power of Giving Up" at www.kylewinkler.org/videos/the-power-of-giving-up.

14

"GOD IS MY VINDICATOR"

*For the L*ORD *will vindicate his people, and
have compassion on his servants.*

—PSALM 135:14

O FTEN ONE OF the greatest obstacles we face is *people*. By this
I mean that the people in our lives, whether friends, family,
coworkers, or strangers, can be some of the greatest sources of
our frustrations, anger, and fear. We allow people to steal our joy
and to control way too much of our lives. People are afraid to go
to a certain kind of church because they worry about what their
family will think. Some are afraid to voice an opinion at work
because of what their coworkers may think. Others are afraid to
be seen with *those* people because of what *these* people will think.

While it is frankly pathetic that we allow the opinion of others
to control so much of our lives, I understand it. I have been there.
Throughout this book you have read about the issues of shyness
and rejection in my childhood and how these plagued me with
years of wrong thinking. The common denominator of all this
was a fear of people—a fear of what they would think of me,
what they might say about me, and how they would treat me.

Ironically, as an adult all the effects of the rejection in my childhood caused me to have an unhealthy desire to please people. I
craved acceptance so badly that I got into a habit of perfectionism
and believed I had to appear the best at everything. When I fell

short or someone disagreed with me, I took it as a deeply personal hit. I would beat myself up if I didn't know the answer to a question, if my words didn't come out perfectly, or if I felt I disappointed someone in some way.

Living so influenced by the opinions of other people is crippling. But eventually I learned about a scripture that began to break the bondage:

> For the LORD will vindicate his people, and have compassion on his servants.
>
> —PSALM 135:14

Perhaps you aren't familiar with the word *vindicate*. It means "to show or prove someone to be right, reasonable, or justified."[1] A person charged with a crime is vindicated when evidence comes forth that he or she is innocent. Someone's criticized views or decisions may be considered vindicated when certain events show they were right.

Psalm 135:14 is significant in that it asserts that it is the Lord who vindicates His people. We don't have to do it ourselves! For too many years I tried to prove or defend myself to get people to like, understand, or support me. But this was exhausting, and more often than not it made things so much worse!

Freshly understanding that God is the vindicator of His people, I began to realize that it is not my job to work so hard to win the approval of others. No, God is the One who causes the right people to accept me. The truth that "God is my vindicator" freed me from the constant striving to be all things to all people, from the exhaustion of trying to get people to understand me, and even from holding myself back in fear of what others might think. Over the years I have learned some important lessons in these areas that I want to share with you throughout the rest of this chapter.

God Causes People to Like You

As you know by now, much of my childhood was characterized by the feeling that nobody liked me. As I grew older, the devil used the rejection of my youth to try to convince me that my life would always be this way. So throughout my teenage years I often walked into social situations believing that I would have to work hard to win the acceptance of others.

Thankfully, from the start of my Christian journey I received great teaching about how to apply God's Word to renew my mind with the truth of what God says about me. In time God's Word, rather than the devil's words, became the lens through which I saw the future. As a result I grew in the boldness and confidence necessary to step into God's call on my life for ministry.

One day within my first couple of years of ministry, I talked to a friend about the people I planned to visit while on a ministry trip. My friend replied, "You have friends everywhere you go!" I thought about those words for a few seconds, and then I praised God. This was the first time I truly realized how much God had turned my situation around. What used to be one of my greatest insecurities is now one of my greatest blessings. I no longer have to strive to get people to like me; relationships just happen organically because of what God has asked me to do.

As I continue being obedient to God's call on my life, I realize that I don't have to change my personality out of fear that people won't like me for who I am. I can just be me, and God works everything else out! This is what Jesus experienced as He grew up doing what He was called to do:

> Jesus increased in wisdom and in stature and in favor with God *and men*.
> —LUKE 2:52, MEV

I must clarify here that God won't cause everyone to like you, just the *right* people. We know that Jesus wasn't liked by everyone, or even the majority of everyone, but God established a support system of the right people around Him to help Him, to encourage Him, and to later advance His message. The Lord will do the same for you. If God is opening a door for a job, ministry, or other opportunity, you can go through it without fear of rejection or having to change who you are to please people. God will give you supernatural favor with the right people to help advance His plans for you.

God Causes People to Understand You

As I mentioned in chapter 9, one of the greatest challenges in my early ministry came when God asked me to leave friends and an area I loved to take a position with a struggling ministry. Significantly adding to the challenge was that I had little to no support for the move from friends and family. In fact, most were very hostile to the idea and accused me of not hearing from God.

In hindsight I understand why people questioned my decision. On paper it looked as if I was committing career suicide at twenty-two years old! Why would I sacrifice so much for what could amount to polishing brass on a sinking ship? Some might have chalked it up to youthful idealism that blinded me to the foolishness of it all. But in this season of transition I was 100 percent sure that I had heard from God.

When you are questioned about something you are sure of, you will likely be tempted to vindicate yourself. I admit, I have often succumbed to such temptation. In these times you think that if other people could know what you know, they would surely come around to understand the reason for your decision. So you try hard to convince them. Unfortunately, as I learned, the more you do this, the crazier people think you are, and thus the more frustrated you become.

Often what God reveals to you in your private, intimate times with Him is not meant to be immediately shared with others. Sometimes it is never meant to be shared with others. God speaks to you in these times to edify you and to build your confidence and courage to step out in obedience. He doesn't necessarily speak to you so that you can use His Words as ammunition to prove yourself when you are questioned or persecuted.

Remember, God is your vindicator—not your words, your wisdom, or your actions. In my case God supernaturally vindicated me just days before I made the move. I will never forget it. A close friend of mine, who at the time was particularly skeptical of my decision, reported to me about a dream she was given the night before. In the dream God gave her a message for me: "Tell Kyle it's time to go." I was amazed! Months of frustration from trying to defend my decision myself was suddenly ended with a single right-on-time dream from the Lord.

Has the Lord whispered something to you that nobody understands? Has He called you to a task that people cannot believe? Welcome to the life of those who truly hear from God! People didn't believe Noah when he spent all those years building a boat in preparation for a worldwide flood. Those closest to Mary couldn't fathom that she remained a virgin, much less that she conceived the Son of God. No amount of persuasion convinced the naysayers. But in each case, God brought vindication through His own supernatural means. Be assured that if God is the One who has spoken to you, He will do the convincing in just the right time!

God Causes People to Support You

Perhaps the most significant source of distress in my early Christianity was the reaction of some of my family to my born-again experience at age sixteen. When I encountered God in a way I never had before, I thought they would celebrate my increased interest in the faith. But I was wrong!

Rather than appreciate my newfound faith, some felt threatened by it. Certainly none of us were prepared to handle it. In their eyes I was the first in the family to stray from a strong denominational heritage, and they couldn't understand my departure. In my zealousness, I tried to cram my faith down their throats and expose everything that I believed was wrong with theirs. Not surprisingly, what ensued were years of tension. They thought I had been brainwashed and had gone off the deep end, and I couldn't understand why nobody would see my relationship with the Lord as something positive.

Fast-forward about eight years to the beginning of my time in seminary. In a course the first semester, I overheard classmates discuss how happy their families were that they were following God's call into ministry. Hearing all this, I began to feel very unsupported and alone in my endeavor. No one held a party for me on the day I revealed that I was attending seminary to pursue ministry. Rather, I was asked questions such as "Why are you doing this?" and "What can you do with that degree?" To be sure, it wasn't that my family was against me, but my path was unfamiliar and they didn't know how to talk about it.

Thankfully, my near decade-long struggle for the support of my family is another example of God's vindication. I can identify a turning point when I learned a different way to talk to them. Rather than being combative or obnoxiously persuasive, God convicted me to use the communication method that Paul used with the Greeks at Athens—to speak to them through the truths of their own faith leaders (Acts 17:28). By my doing so, this took my family off of the defense, which allowed them to truly see the fruit of God's work in my life over time.

Shortly after this turning point I began to notice that my family took more interest in my work. Eventually they asked more substantive questions, respected me as an authority in the faith, and even came to attend my speaking engagements in their area. Most importantly, this opened some of them to personally encounter God in their own ways.

Today my family members are some of my greatest supporters and often share the content that I produce with their friends and on social media. Even if they still don't understand everything I do, I know that I have their support and I feel celebrated in my calling. To be sure, though I certainly made adjustments in how I related to them, the majority of their support came through nothing short of the supernatural vindication of God.

Perhaps you are in similar tensions with your loved ones. Whether about faith, education, career, or relationships, we all want to feel supported by those we cherish. Certainly I can't guarantee you will experience this overnight. There are often many ways the Lord needs to work on people—including yourself— before you realize the support for which you pray. But as I learned, it is often when you stop arguing that the Lord starts to do the talking. Be encouraged: God will do in ten seconds what you can't do in ten years of defending or persuading. Your vindication will come, and it will be worth the wait.

Shake It Off!

After I first encountered God as a teenager, there was no warm-up period for me; I was immediately consumed with the things of God and wanted everything He had to offer. I quickly learned, however, that not everyone shared or appreciated my passion. I understood why the unsaved might consider me strange, but it was the accusations of fellow Christians that especially hurt. For a long time I couldn't understand why someone who claims to be a follower of Jesus would think that talking about God is radical or that the supernatural is crazy, or why a professing Jesus follower would criticize the ways someone tries to live a life that is pleasing to God.

Even shortly before writing this, someone told me about a comment they overheard about how "weird" it is that I talk so much about the Lord. When I sought God about this, I heard Him say, "Let them think you are too radical or too different. There is a reason why I chose you for such a time as this, and it is definitely not because you are like everyone else." Perhaps you should also hear those words for yourself!

Understandably, none of us enjoys criticism. But today accusations about the intensity of my faith, which used to unnerve me, become more and more like a badge of honor to me. As Christians we are declared by God to be holy, which means to be set apart. And so by default, a passionate Christian should seem weird to others who aren't serving God with passion. And that is a good thing!

Finally, you must be realistic that not everyone will like you, understand you, or support you, and that is OK. It won't matter what you do or say; for whatever reason—perhaps because of jealousy, insecurity, or just the way you look—some people will never appreciate the great person you are! To deal with these kinds of people, Jesus told His disciples to "shake off the dust from your feet" and move on (Matt. 10:14). Don't waste time trying so hard to win the approval of others. When people don't understand you, when they wrongly accuse you, or when they mock you, *shake it off!* Be content that you are accepted and favored by God. He is your vindicator, and He will give you favor with the right people, in the right places, and at the right times.*

#ActivateTheWord
God is my vindicator.

My worth is not in the acceptance of people but in being accepted by God. I am not bothered when people misunderstand me, when they don't like me, or when they criticize me. In His timing, God will clear my name; He will prove that I am sincere. I trust that God is changing hearts and am thankful that He gives me favor with the right people, in the right places, and at the right times.

---

* Go Beyond the Book: Watch my short teaching titled "Overcoming 'People Problems'" at www.kylewinkler.org/videos/overcoming-people-problems.

15

"GOD PROVIDES FOR ALL MY NEEDS"

And my God will fully satisfy every need of yours according to his riches in glory in Christ Jesus.

—PHILIPPIANS 4:19

THE SHUT UP, Devil! mobile app was my first major ministry project—and my first major lesson about God's provision. When God began to speak to me about the concept, I had only recently launched the ministry and had next to nothing in my bank account. With the Lord's direction I proceeded to get quotes for the cost of its development. The best estimate was in the thousands. Though I didn't know where the money would come from, I felt strongly that I should proceed in faith.

Giving the OK to start the project was the easy part. Stepping out in faith is not so difficult when no initial payment is due. The worries begin when the bills start to come in. After a few months the development costs started to mount, and anxiety about how I would pay the bills started to consume my mind. I protested to God, "If you don't provide by X date, I am quitting the ministry! I just can't keep doing this!"

I know that I just revealed a lack of faith that is not exemplary, but God's provision is. A couple of months after development began, I introduced the project to the people in some churches where I was speaking. I didn't tell the congregations the exact amount I needed, but the collections they took up exactly covered the bills. Of course I was relieved!

Several months later the app was released, and since then it has helped tens of thousands of people overcome the threats and lies of the enemy. But ironically, well before the app had an impact on anyone else, it first helped to teach me an important lesson, a lesson it was crucial to learn at the start of the ministry: *what God orders, He pays for.*

God Will Satisfy Every Need

Some have counted at least 169 verses in the Bible that describe the ways God promises to provide. Of these verses, perhaps the most popular is Paul's words to the church at Philippi:

> And my God will fully satisfy every need of yours according to his riches in glory in Christ Jesus.
>
> —Philippians 4:19

We must recognize that Paul wasn't instituting a new promise here. Rather, he was standing on the age-old promise of God's provision dating as far back as when Abraham named God "Jehovah Jireh," which means "the Lord will provide."

Given Paul's situation, the Philippian believers surely took notice of his words. Paul was once a high-ranking member of the Jewish establishment: "a pure-blooded citizen of Israel and a member of the tribe of Benjamin," in fact (Phil. 3:5, NLT). Yet for the cause of Christ he was willing to walk away from his heritage and start over.

Though perhaps Paul started over with nothing, he didn't remain with nothing. As he continued to serve Jesus, Paul experienced the faithfulness of God to meet his needs and boasted at times even to have more than enough (Phil. 4:18). In deconstructing Paul's declaration of God's provision, we can learn a great deal about how God intends to provide for us too.

"And my God"

Paul began his assurance not by generally referring to God, but by personalizing God as "my God." By doing so, he essentially encouraged the people, "Look at my life. If there's anyone who knows about the fear of not having food, water, or a place to live, it's me! Yet here I am—content and joyful! The same God who takes care of me will also take care of you." Here again, God shows no favoritism. Paul's God is your God and my God, and He will fully provide for you and me just the same as He provided for Paul.

"Will fully satisfy"

There is no wiggle room for doubt here. God won't hold out on us; He won't give to us partially and leave us needing more. No, Paul reveals the guarantee that the God who calls you knows the needs of your call. God is ready and able to supply the whole kit and caboodle, right down to the last cent. And often God will also leave some to spare as a blessing for your obedience.

"Every need of yours"

A need is considered something that is essential to accomplish a certain purpose. Of course, to maintain life, we have certain needs, most obviously food, water, and shelter. Some other life needs are emotional, such as the needs for acceptance, love, and value. You will also have needs according to the vocation to which God has called you. To raise a family, for example, you must have the means to support your family. Or if God has called you to full-time ministry, you will have other definite needs that require fulfillment.

Here Paul assures that just as God has always done for His people, God will provide for your every need. But you must be careful not to confuse a need with a want. Wants are often luxuries, which would be nice to have but are not crucial to the mission. As we will learn below, if they are not harmful to your overall well-being and purpose, God delights in blessing you with your wants. But unlike a need, He doesn't promise to provide them.

"According to His riches in glory"

God doesn't provide for your every need *out* of His riches but *according* to them. The difference is significant. If He provided *out* of His riches, it would indicate a supply that might eventually be depleted (even if it is a huge supply). And thus you might fear that God doesn't have enough left for you. But fear not: God keeps no inventory on His provisions; they never run out. And He hasn't given the answer to your financial need, miracle, or breakthrough to someone else.

God's provision "according to His riches" also means that it is not according to anything of yours. That is, God supplies according to His mercy, grace, and unconditional love, not according to your perfect behavior. I know many people who believe they have lack in an area because God is upset with them about something. Know that the Bible promises that God holds no good thing back from His children (Ps. 84:11). He is not a Father who threatens, "Do this or else!" If provision were dependent on upholding some sort of law or living perfectly, we would all be vagabonds. Thankfully, God meets our needs according to the glory of who He is, not according to what we do, which is precisely why we can count on it.

"In Christ Jesus"

Finally, Paul directs us to the signature on the check of the promise: "in Christ Jesus." Jesus's name is always the guarantor of any of God's promises. To see if God has the "credit" to make such a guarantee, consider that He owns everything (Ps. 24:1)! The resources of heaven and earth are at His disposal, which means He is able to provide for you. But to see if God is willing, you need to look no further than Christ on the cross. God's sacrifice of His only Son demonstrates the extreme lengths He is willing to go to provide what you need.

Don't Beg God for Your Needs

I remember another time when I was stressing over some personal bills that seemed to be accumulating with no end in sight. My mind went into overdrive, creating worrisome, hypothetical situations that nearly crippled me with fear and caused me to beg, "God, *please* provide!" Thankfully, not long into my rant, God spoke to me. "This isn't your problem; it's Mine," the Lord assured. And then He directed me to the words of Jesus:

> Do not worry about your life, what you will eat or what
> you will drink, or about your body, what you will wear. Is
> not life more than food, and the body more than clothing?
> Look at the birds of the air; they neither sow nor reap nor
> gather into barns, and yet your heavenly Father feeds them.
> Are you not of more value than they?
>
> —MATTHEW 6:25–26

More than anything else in creation, you and I are God's priority because we are His children and He is our Father. And as a good Father, God is never delinquent in His fatherly responsibilities to provide.

As God revealed to me, your needs are not your problem! And you don't have to beg or plead with Him to provide for them. If a thing is necessary for life or essential to something He has asked you to do, then God wants you to be assured of His promise to provide it. Your only responsibility in God's provision is to look to Him above all things. As you keep your eyes on Him, He will keep His hand of provision on you (Matt. 6:33). No begging is necessary—only trust and obedience.

Why God Wants to Bless You

For whatever reason, some people are hostile to the idea that God wants to bless His people. Instead, they think that holiness and poverty go hand in hand. But this is a deception of the enemy!

The devil loves for Christians to remain in financial struggle or to just get by because it keeps us focused only on ourselves.

God sometimes calls us into difficult situations, which He uses to shape us for the better. And we all know that He doesn't always give us what we want. But we shouldn't have a mind-set that God is withholding anything we need or that He wants us to remain in difficulty forever. No, all throughout the Bible we see that it is prosperity and well-being—not poverty and struggle—that God ultimately desires for His people. Read what God says:

> This book of the law shall not depart out of your mouth; you shall meditate on it day and night....For then you shall make your way prosperous, and then you shall be successful.
>
> —JOSHUA 1:8

> Happy are those... [whose] delight is in the law of the LORD, and on his law they meditate day and night. They are like trees planted by streams of water, which yield their fruit in its season, and their leaves do not wither. In all that they do, they prosper.
>
> —PSALM 1:1–3

> Great is the LORD, who delights in the welfare of his servant.
>
> —PSALM 35:27

> And God is able to provide you with every blessing in abundance, so that by always having enough of everything, you may share abundantly in every good work.
>
> —2 CORINTHIANS 9:8

Yes, these scriptures are clear that God not only promises to meet our needs, but that He also delights to bless us far and above what we need. And He does so for at least a couple of reasons.

God blesses us to be a blessing.

When God called Abraham, He promised that He would establish a great nation out of him. He then promised to bless

Abraham and this nation so that they would be a blessing to others (Gen. 12:2).

God blesses us for the same purpose—to be a blessing to others. He never blesses us so that we will hoard possessions. He doesn't want us to hold onto His blessings with clenched hands, but to hold them lightly with open palms. And that is an important word picture to understand. Clenched hands can hold only so much, and they can't continue to receive. But open palms allow gifts to continue to come in and go out, which makes you a flowing river of blessings. Through this posture, not only are your needs met, but also you get the joy of being part of God meeting the needs of other people.

To understand the purpose of prosperity, consider what God has done through America's abundance. In less than two hundred years of independence, America rose to have incredible wealth. But its wealth wasn't meant for materialism and greed. No, God had plans for the wealth of America as a funding source for the gospel around the world. And that is what happened.

Many of the most longstanding and recognizable international Christian institutions, such as Campus Crusade for Christ, Wycliffe Bible Translators, and the Billy Graham Evangelistic Association, were all originally financed as a result of Americans' prosperity.[1] The surplus of blessed people is also largely responsible for the pioneering of Christian media networks, the largest of which now has the potential to reach hundreds of millions in every region of the world, every day.[2] Additionally, it is reported that Americans give more than $115 billion per year to religious groups, which contribute to church plants, discipleship, and mission work both at home and abroad.[3] Certainly I don't cite all of this to brag on America, but to demonstrate the positive effects of purposeful prosperity.

If you want the prosperity of God, you must show that you can handle it. And being a cheapskate isn't going to do it! Begin by giving to others. As you give, God will be faithful to replenish. Yes, He will bless you to be a blessing.

God blesses us to draw others to Him.

When God spoke to Moses at the burning bush, He reminded him of His covenant to bring Israel to "their own fertile and spacious land...a land flowing with milk and honey" (Exod. 3:8, NLT). God's desire for His people wasn't just to meet their need for land, but to bless them with more than enough. A bit later God further explained His reasoning to Moses:

> Listen, I am making a covenant with you in the presence of all your people. I will perform miracles that have never been performed anywhere in all the earth or in any nation. And all the people around you will see the power of the LORD— the awesome power I will display for you.
>
> —EXODUS 34:10, NLT

Part of the miracle power that God promised to display for His people was the power of His provision. God wanted other nations to marvel at and envy how much the God of Israel blessed His people so that in their amazement they might want to serve Him too.

Likewise, the blessings in your life should direct people to the God who provides those blessings. To be sure, people won't be attracted to God by greediness, stinginess, or stress. No, people will see the God of your prosperity by the peace through which you live and the cheerfulness through which you give.

More Ways Than Money

Perhaps you have heard the popular parable about the man stuck on his rooftop during a flood. After he prayed to God for help, a man in a rowboat came to offer to take him to safety. But the stranded man declined the offer by shouting back, "No, thanks. I believe God will save me." After this a motorboat came by, but still the man declined to jump in for the same reason. Finally, a helicopter flew in, but again the stranded man refused to get on board, still holding to his belief that God would save him.

Unfortunately, the waters continued to rise and the stranded man drowned. When he got to heaven, he had the opportunity to discuss the situation with God. "I had faith in You, but You didn't save me," the man complained. "Why did You let me down?" To this God replied, "I sent you a rowboat, a motorboat, and a helicopter. What more did you expect?"

This story provides insight into the ways God provides and blesses. Similar to the stranded man, we often expect God to meet our needs in a certain way, which is likely monetarily. If the provision doesn't come in this way, we are then tempted to feel that God didn't uphold His promise. But God has more than one way to bless and provide. Yes, for some God richly provides through a well-paying job or some financial favor. For others He provides through other means, such as gifts from other believers. I have even experienced God's provision through the blessing of friendship. During a period of a couple of years when I didn't have health insurance, at least two situations arose that required emergency attention. Thankfully, years before, the Lord connected me with a physician who became my best friend. In these situations my friend was kind enough to perform the procedures I needed, which saved me thousands.

When Israel needed deliverance from captivity in Egypt, God raised up Moses to bring them out. Through a rock God provided His people with water. Out of thin air God faithfully delivered food each morning to His people in the middle of the desert. Provision might come in the most unconventional or unlikely ways, but be assured that it will come.*

---

* Go Beyond the Book: Watch my short teaching titled "Don't Beg God for Your Needs" at www.kylewinkler.org/videos/dont-beg-god-for-your-needs.

#ActivateTheWord
God provides for all my needs.

I will not worry about what I will eat, drink, or wear, or how I will pay the bills. God knows what I require, and He will supply it all according to His riches in glory in Christ. As I am obedient and faithful to handle God's provision, I believe He will generously bless me beyond my needs so that I can also be a blessing to others.

16

"I AM HEALED"

*He himself bore our sins in his body on the cross,
so that, free from sins, we might live for righteousness; by his wounds you have been healed.*

—1 PETER 2:24

WHETHER OR NOT it is always God's will to heal is the source of tremendous debate. Most who object to the idea that it is always God's will to heal do so based on apparent reality. We know that not everyone who prays for healing recovers in the ways for which they pray. Thus some people conclude that it isn't always God's will to heal.

We have to be careful not to draw conclusions about the will of God based on bad experiences. Bad things happen all the time that God doesn't desire. For example, God says that it is His will that no one dies without first coming to salvation; yet unfortunately, unsaved people continue to die every day (2 Pet. 3:9). The earthly reality of something doesn't change God's will. No, we must understand that most often something else is at work.

Consider the following illustration. If you walk into a junk-yard, you will see piles of old, dilapidated, and wrecked vehicles. It would be unthinkable to ask, "Why did the manufacturers create these vehicles like that?" Clearly they didn't. The manu-facturers created these vehicles in pristine condition with abso-lutely no intention that any would end up demolished. Blaming the manufacturers for the final condition of the vehicles would be foolish. The problem is obvious: somebody wrecked them.

In the same way, we shouldn't look at the awful experiences of life—suffering, sickness, disease, and death—and blame them on the will of the Creator. The devastation we see today was never the intention of God but is the result of a reckless driver named Satan and a visual impairment called sin.

Divine Health: God's Will From the Beginning

To understand God's will with regard to health, we first need to go back to the beginning. Throughout His creation of the heavens and the earth, God stood back six times to marvel at what He had done and saw it as "good" (Gen. 1:4, 10, 12, 18, 21, 25). When all was finished, the Bible records that "God saw everything that he had made, and indeed, it was *very good*" (Gen. 1:31). Surely God would not have pronounced everything in creation as "very good" if some very bad things such as disease and death were already present.

God's proclamation that His original creation was "very good" means that He created it perfect. Of course, we should expect nothing less than a perfect creation by a perfect Creator. The Bible further describes what God's original creation was like. It was a place inhabited by His presence and therefore free from the contamination of evil. It was also a place of complete provision. Adam and Eve didn't have to work for anything but solely depended on God for their needs. Finally, creation was a place free from death. Accordingly there was no sickness, disease, or infirmity of any kind.

So what happened? In a word—sin. From the beginning God warned the first couple that if they ate fruit from the "tree of the knowledge of good and evil," they would then experience death (Gen. 2:16–17). And that is precisely what happened. With disobedience to God, Adam and Eve brought sin and all its ugliness into God's perfect world.

Healing: The Main Ministry of Jesus

Well before the creation of the world, God had a plan in place to restore what would be lost should humankind fall into sin. That plan was Jesus (1 Pet. 1:20). The Bible tells us that Jesus entered this world for a single purpose: "to destroy the works of the devil" (1 John 3:8). That is, everything Jesus did through His ministry was meant to begin a restoration back to how it was in the beginning. In chapter 20, we will explore all the ways Jesus did this. But for now I want to focus on just one of the primary effects of Christ's ministry: Jesus came to defeat sickness and disease, to restore the health of God's people.

Just after Jesus selected His first disciples, He entered Galilee where He went about "proclaiming the good news of the kingdom and curing every disease and every sickness among the people" (Matt. 4:23). This was the main theme of His ministry. In fact, Matthew chose to reiterate this again in his Gospel, as did Luke in the Book of Acts (Matt. 9:35; Acts 10:38).

Let's look a bit more closely at the two main tenets of Jesus's ministry. First, what is the "good news of the kingdom"? Jesus answers this question in what He tells John the Baptist's messengers to report about His ministry:

> "Go and tell John what you hear and see: the blind receive their sight, the lame walk, the lepers are cleansed, the deaf hear, the dead are raised, and the poor have good news brought to them."
>
> —MATTHEW 11:4–5

What we see here is that Jesus made His ministry about proclaiming the news that the infirmities that cause blindness, lameness, deafness, and death stand no chance in His presence. Simply put, Jesus's words serve as a heads-up to the devil that God's will for health is being restored.

The second part of Jesus's proclamation is all about application. That is, Jesus didn't just talk about healing; He did it! And it should be noted that He didn't cure just some diseases and sicknesses, but He cured *every one* of them. There is not one instance in the New Testament in which Jesus refused someone who needed healing. He never said, "No, I'm sorry. God wants you to have this affliction, so you must always suffer with it." Even in answering His disciples' questions about why certain people are born with defects, Jesus reiterated God's will to heal: "He was born blind so that God's works might be revealed in him" (John 9:3).

Finally, healing was so prominent in Jesus's ministry that it was the reason He was put to death. John's Gospel records that when Jesus went to Jerusalem, He healed a man who lay ill for thirty-eight years at the pool of Bethesda. That Jesus healed this man is not surprising. The scandal is that Jesus healed Him on the Sabbath—a day on which the Jewish leaders forbade any such activity. John is then very clear that it was Jesus's decision to heal on the Sabbath that began the religious leaders' persecution of Him, which ultimately ended in His crucifixion (John 5:16).

The How, Where, and When of Healing

That Jesus was willing to die so that people would be healed is precisely what the prophet Isaiah foretold and what Peter affirmed actually happened.

> But he was wounded for our transgressions, crushed for our iniquities; upon him was the punishment that made us whole, and by his bruises we are healed.
>
> —ISAIAH 53:5

> He himself bore our sins in his body on the cross, so that, free from sins, we might live for righteousness; by his wounds you have been healed.
>
> —1 PETER 2:24

Though some believe these references only suggest spiritual healing, on deeper inspection it is clear that the Bible intends to mean physical healing as well.

Consider that the word Isaiah uses for *healing* is *rapha*, which is the same word by which God's people named Him, Jehovah Rapha—the Lord who heals.[1] And they didn't only mean that God heals spiritually, but throughout the Old Testament Jehovah Rapha attributed to every kind of healing—spiritual, emotional, *and* physical (Ps. 103:3; Isa. 30:26; Jer. 30:17). Additionally, in the New Testament Matthew's report that Jesus "cured all who were sick" is used by him to celebrate the fulfillment of Isaiah's prophecy (Matt. 8:16–17).

Both Isaiah and Peter indicate that physical healing was a primary purpose for Christ's death on the cross. And their words tell us about three very important aspects of healing: how Jesus healed, where Jesus healed, and when Jesus healed.

How Jesus healed

To understand how Jesus healed, we must first know the traditional Jewish beliefs about sickness. We can get a glimpse into this from the disciples' question to Jesus about the man born blind. They asked, "Rabbi, who sinned, this man or his parents, that he was born blind?" (John 9:2). In other words, because there was no sickness until after sin entered creation, the Jewish people concluded sickness was always a result of one's immediate sin, either of themselves or their parents.

In this they were partially right. As I said earlier, sickness is a consequence of sin. Still, as Jesus further explained, one's sickness is not necessarily the direct result of his or her personal sin or the parents' sin. Rather, sickness is the general outcome of sin at work in the fallen world.

Nonetheless, since God's covenant with Abraham, God's people trusted that He would take sickness away from them (Exod. 23:25). They praised Him for His benefits, which included the forgiveness of sin, and thus the healing of all diseases (Ps. 103:3).

Knowing all this, we can see why Jesus's healings were so controversial to the Jewish religious leaders of His day. Being physically healed was the indication of the forgiveness of sins. This of course was an act that only God could perform. So Jesus's healings confronted them with the truth that He was God in the flesh—a truth they refused to accept.

What the religious leaders didn't realize is that Jesus's death wouldn't stop this newfound healing awakening. Instead, it would bring it to its climax. You see, in God's law a sacrifice of a pure, spotless lamb was essential for the forgiveness of sin (Heb. 9:22). But God never meant for this practice to last forever. No, the animal sacrifices were intended to be a foreshadowing of the ultimate sacrifice of Christ on the cross. That is, Jesus was the pure, sinless Lamb, sacrificed on the altar of Calvary for the once-and-for-all forgiveness of whoever would later accept His sacrifice. Therefore, the question of how Jesus healed is answered by the shedding of His blood brought forth "by His bruises," which provided the removal of sin, resulting in the restoration of God's original will of health and healing for His people.

Where Jesus healed

Notice that in the three Gospel accounts of Jesus healing the man who was paralyzed, He began by forgiving the man of his sins (Matt. 9:1–8; Mark 2:1–12; Luke 5:17–26). "Take heart, son; your sins are forgiven," He assured the paralyzed man (Matt. 9:2). Then Jesus declared, "Stand up, take your bed and go to your home" (Matt. 9:6). In this, Jesus's earthly ministry of healing was a foreshadowing of His finished work on the cross. Yes, the cross where Jesus ultimately forgave our sins is also the place where He ultimately provided for our healing.

When Jesus healed

Isaiah noted, "By his bruises we are healed," and Peter similarly declared, "By his wounds you have been healed" (Isa. 53:5; 1 Pet. 2:24). Neither refers to a healing that might take place but to a healing that has already happened.

Indeed, more than two thousand years ago, when Jesus

thundered His final words from the cross, "It is finished," He declared that the works of the devil were now finished in the lives of God's people (John 19:30). As with the forgiveness of sins, our healing, once and for all, was paid for by His blood sacrifice at Calvary. This means that God doesn't still heal today—He *already* healed!

How to Activate Divine Healing

Did I get your attention with what I just said? Please don't confuse me with those who believe God no longer performs miracles today. I am far from that! I can say with certainty that people still experience healing today. And when naysayers try to tell me otherwise, I let them know that they should bark up a different tree because I am too far gone. I have been there when deaf ears were opened. I have seen the paralyzed miraculously walk. I was beside a friend's mother when pain from metal rods in her neck instantly went away. Nobody can convince me that divine healing isn't for today: I have seen too much!

In the occasions of miraculous healing I have encountered, you might be surprised to hear that none happened because of a cautious, insecure prayer, such as "Dear most gracious heavenly Father, we come before You today to ask for Your hand of healing on our sister...if it be Thy will." No, divine healing happens when you are confident that God already decided to heal and you activate His healing by speaking it in faith over situations, symptoms, or body parts. Call out the issue by name and command it to go in Jesus's name. The declaration at the end of this chapter is a great way to start.

I know that this is uncomfortable for some. Perhaps it might even seem irreverent. But this isn't just my theory of healing. It is modeled by Jesus and by those throughout the New Testament. Jesus never prayed to ask God to heal someone. Rather, in every instance, He *declared* healing upon them:

> [Jesus] stretched out his hand and touched [the leper], saying, "I do choose. Be made clean!"
>
> —Matthew 8:3

> [Jesus] said to the paralytic—"I say to you, stand up, take your mat and go to your home."
>
> —Mark 2:10–11

> Jesus said to [the blind man], "Receive your sight; your faith has saved you."
>
> —Luke 18:42

Of course, some argue that Jesus could speak in this way because He is God. But notice Jesus's directions as He sent out His twelve disciples to preach about the kingdom. "Heal the sick, raise the dead, cleanse lepers, cast out demons," He instructed (Matt. 10:8, esv). He said the same to seventy others (Luke 10:9). And the early disciples took this to heart. As his first recorded act of healing, Peter spoke healing over a man who was crippled. "Stand up and walk," he asserted (Acts 3:6). James instructed the early church to pray a "prayer of faith" over the sick and they *will* recover (James 5:15).

You and I are also tasked to continue Jesus's ministry to heal the sick. We don't need to ask God for the power to do so. No, the power is already available through the work of the cross, which is received in faith by activating the power of God's Word in the name of Jesus.

What If I Am Not Healed?

If it is God's will to heal, then what do we say about the reality that some people of faith get sick and don't recover? Do these people not have enough faith? Not necessarily. There are a variety of reasons why people might not be healed in the way they would like, and lack of faith is only one reason.

First, we must realize that while healing can and does sometimes happen instantly, more often than not, it is a process. We even see this process in Jesus's ministry. In one account where

Jesus healed a blind man, it took Him two attempts before the man could fully see (Mark 8:22–25). In another story detailing Jesus's healing of ten lepers, they weren't healed on the spot but "as they went" (Luke 17:11–14).

Second, it shouldn't seem like a cop-out to believe that passing on from this world is the ultimate healing. The everlasting life received at salvation gives each of us a life that never ends. Sure, your location will one day change and you will then shed your earthly body, but only for the better. It should be great news to hear that *you* will always exist, but eventually in an eternally healed state. This is why Paul remarked, "To die is gain" (Phil. 1:21, MEV).

Whatever the situation, never accept that healing isn't God's will just because it doesn't happen instantly. Rather, from the moment healing is declared on yourself or someone else, trust that it is received and begin to thank God for it. For as long as it takes, remain standing on the truth of God's Word about His will for healing. Then trust God's timing for the results.*

#ActivateTheWord
I am healed.

On the cross Jesus bore my sins and shed His blood for my complete healing. Therefore, my body must come into alignment with the truth of God's Word. Sickness and disease have no place in me—they must go. I declare that I am made well in Jesus's name.

---

* Go Beyond the Book: Watch my short teaching titled "Activate Your Healing" at www.kylewinkler.org/videos/activate-your-healing.

PART FIVE

STRATEGIC DECLARATIONS TO WIN SPIRITUAL BATTLES

17

"I AM MORE THAN A CONQUEROR"

In all these things we are more than conquerors through him who loved us.

—ROMANS 8:37

WE CHRISTIANS SHOULDN'T be surprised that the devil is the orchestrator of many of our struggles. Paul revealed that our battles are not with flesh and blood, but "against the spiritual forces of evil in the heavenly places" (Eph. 6:12). Yet for too many the thought of something sinister behind our troubles is revolutionary. In our secular society many learn that the devil is nothing more than a character in ancient folklore—from a day void of modern science. Accordingly, the effects and symptoms of spiritual battles are often explained away with psychology.

Unfortunately, this idea has also crept into the modern church, where Christians are increasingly being taught that the devil, demons, and hell don't exist. Even those who acknowledge Satan's existence often don't want to get too specific about him or his ways, out of fear that such teaching might incite paranoia or sound too negative. Could there be a more effective deception to hold people hostage? Certainly disbelief in the devil doesn't change the reality of his existence. It only keeps people ignorant of his devices and in bondage to his every whim.

As the world seems to spin out of control with more disaster, scandal, terror, and heartache, it is time to take off our rose-colored glasses and see much of these for what they are. People today need to be alerted to the truth that the struggles they face might not be the product of happenstance, unbalanced chemicals in the brain, or the weather. No, these just might be part of a plot by an enemy so threatened by our destinies that he seeks to take us down.

But plots are often foiled! You don't have to be a doormat to Satan's devices any longer. Keep reading to learn how it is possible to stand up to your greatest foe and ensure an overwhelming victory against whatever he launches at you.

The Lion on the Prowl

When facing any opponent, the better you understand your rival, the better your chances for victory. The devil knows who you are, and he studies you to devise the most effective plan of attack. Your success in facing and overcoming his attacks begins by understanding how he works.

Thankfully the Bible gives plenty of insight into the devil and his schemes. One of the most revealing illustrations is Peter's likening of Satan to a "roaring lion."

> Stay alert! Watch out for your great enemy, the devil. He prowls around like a roaring lion, looking for someone to devour.
> —1 PETER 5:8, NLT

The image Peter gives here is definitely not coincidental. Those who know much about how a lion hunts understand that this description is intentionally worded to teach us how Satan operates and what we should expect from him. Let's look at this passage.

Relative to the size of its body, a lion has a small heart and lungs. Thus the lion is not a fast runner, nor does it have the stamina to run for long periods of time. In fact, a lion's speed maxes out at about fifty miles per hour and occurs only in short bursts.[1]

Therefore, because the majority of its prey can outrun it, the lion takes a unique approach to hunting—it prowls and stalks.

Not surprisingly, the majority of a lion's successful hunts happen in the cover of night, when its soon-to-be victim can't see it approaching. Once the lion has worked its way close enough, it charges its target from an angle that is out of sight, jumps on top to wrestle it to the ground, and then finishes it off with a bite to the throat or by covering its mouth to suffocate it.[2]

The parallels to the works of Satan aren't difficult to see. The enemy spends much time throughout your life studying you to discover your weaknesses. He then waits for those moments when your guard is down to suddenly and forcefully move in for the kill.

The Common Attacks of the Enemy

Just before he described the devil like a roaring lion, Peter said, "Stay alert!" This is very important to thwarting an attack. In nature an animal's awareness of its surroundings and potential enemies is essential for its safety. And that is true for us spiritually. Paul thus urged us to be familiar with Satan's evil schemes "so that we may not be outwitted" (2 Cor. 2:11).

In his letter to the Romans, Paul alerted us to Satan's common devices: accusations, condemnation, tribulation, distress, persecution, famine, nakedness, danger, and sword (Rom. 8:31–35). As we will see below, each of these has its own set of symptoms and outcomes. Understanding these will help you know how to counter the attacks on your life.

Because of the nature of this book, I realize that you might be reading this chapter first or before some of the others. Throughout the previous chapters, we explored the solutions to each of the attacks listed below. With each I have referenced the corresponding chapter you can later turn to for specific help.

Accusations or condemnation

The Bible refers to the devil as "the accuser of our brothers and sisters" (Rev. 12:10, NLT). Understand that the devil isn't so much after those who are in the world; he already has them. Instead, he is after those of us in the faith who are a threat to him. Using reminders of the past, Satan accuses and condemns Christians to make us believe we aren't good enough to serve God. Likewise, when Satan tempts us, his goal is to lure us to give in to a weakness so that he can later convince us that we aren't deserving of God's love and forgiveness.

 See chapter 6: "I am loved unconditionally."

Tribulation

Tribulation is the "state of great trouble or suffering." [3] None of us is immune from it. In fact, Jesus assured that all believers would face times such as these at various moments in life (John 16:33). To be sure, tribulation is a natural result of a fallen world or even consequences of our own actions. Still, the devil also concocts tribulations, which might include physical illness, abuse, or unjust treatment. While tribulations can be excruciating, they have boundaries and expiration dates. Satan gets mileage out of these attacks by causing you to question God's goodness out of the belief that He is afflicting you because He is mad at you.

 See chapter 12: "Something good will happen to me."

Distress

Distress is made up of two parts: *di* and *stress*. Thus it literally means "to be doubly stressed to the point of extreme anxiety, sorrow, or pain." To put it simply, distress is the ultimate feeling of being trapped in a hopeless situation. The devil will cause distress over troubled relationships, jobs, and addictions. He will tell you there is no way out or that the situation will never change. Symptoms of a distress attack include physical or mental fatigue, depression, lack of motivation, and even suicidal thoughts.

See chapter 11: "The joy of the Lord is my strength."

Persecution

If someone has mocked you for your faith, then you have been persecuted. We have all likely experienced this to some degree. Those of us in the West can't fathom the persecution many around the world endure—unspeakable acts of violence that unfortunately often end in death. Throughout the years Satan has induced times of extreme persecution in hopes of stomping out the faith. Thankfully, he fails every time. But he doesn't learn. The devil still brings about harassment or intimidation—by friends, family, coworkers, or complete strangers—to shut you up.

 See chapter 14: "God is my vindicator."

Famine or nakedness

Both famine and nakedness represent a "lack attack." The devil sometimes tries to cut off your financial supply by bringing about situations that devour your resources: constant vehicle repairs, medical issues, or even temptations toward undisciplined spending. Satan's goal in all this is to occupy you with worry that your needs won't be met or to convince you to look to other "providers" instead of to God.

 See chapter 15: "God provides for all my needs."

Danger or sword

Finally, danger and sword represent the possibility of suffering or harm. As we have learned, the devil is a master at using circumstances and unknowns to build imaginations of danger in our minds. The symptoms of this include paralyzing fear and worry intended to hold you back from steps of faith or obedience to God.

 See chapter 9: "I don't worry about anything."

More Than Conquerors

Paul's list of Satan's strangleholds was never meant to incite paranoia in believers. He didn't intend for it to cause us to huddle in isolation so that we are never messed with by the devil. Quite the opposite actually. He concluded his list by offering assurance:

> No, in all these things we are more than conquerors through him who loved us.
>
> —Romans 8:37

Here Paul urged us not to be afraid because in Christ we are given victory over all these things: the enemy, each attack on the list above, and every derivative of these attacks. But that is just the beginning. Fascinatingly, Paul used two Greek words to form one word that is not used anywhere else in the Bible—*hypernikaō*. The first part, *huper*, means "over, beyond, or above."[4] The second part, *nikaō*, means to "conquer, prevail, or overcome."[5] These parts combined, this word is translated as "more than conquerors."[6]

To be a conqueror seems great enough. But by joining the two words together, Paul made a tremendous statement about you and me. Essentially, by calling us "more than conquerors," he is saying this:

- "We are greater conquerors, superior conquerors, higher and better conquerors!"

- "We are more than a match for any foe!"

- "We are utmost conquerors, paramount conquerors, top-notch conquerors, unsurpassed conquerors, unequaled and unrivaled conquerors!"[7]

How awesome! But there is more! The present and active tense of the word indicates that not only are we super conquerors in the here and now, but we are also victorious forever into the future. Victory has no expiration date!

How is this possible? "*Through* him who loved us" (Rom. 8:37).

Victory over all the things listed in the Romans 8 passage isn't accomplished out of your own merits or efforts. That is, victory is achieved not by what you do but by what Jesus did. His victory is your victory! Sure, you might be faced with the devil's attacks from time to time. But standing in the truths of Jesus's love demonstrated on the cross will hold you in constant victory far above the influence of Satan's assaults.

How to Conquer an Attack

Let's return now to the illustration of Satan as a roaring lion. The three steps wildlife experts say are essential to overcoming a physical assault by a lion also provide insight into how to victoriously *stand* against the devil.

Stay calm.

When a lion prepares to attack, he lets out a ground-shaking roar that will reverberate through your very core. Undoubtedly this will sound terrifying! But experts claim that how you would want to react in this instance is the opposite of what you should do. That is, rather than bolting to escape in a panic, remaining calm and thinking clearly could save your life.[8]

Remember, Peter not only likened Satan to a lion, but he said that he is a "roaring lion" (1 Pet. 5:8). The devil's roars consist of threats, lies, and accusations related to the common attacks listed above. They might sound something like this:

- *Threat:* "If you step out to do that, I will expose all your dirty secrets and nobody will ever trust you."

- *Lie:* "The road ahead is too difficult; you should give up now."

- *Accusation:* "Look at all your failures; God is disgusted with you."

Roars such as these have tremendous power to evoke overwhelming fear and cause you to retreat, which is just what the devil wants. When you feel the ground shake beneath you, your heart pounds, and your feelings say, "Run!," staying calm is a key component to your victory. But how is this possible?

A sure way to stay calm is to think clearly. You can do this by bringing to mind the ultimate demonstration of the One who loves you. Meditate on the benefits of the cross—that you are forgiven, healed, made brand new, and reconciled by God, to name a few. The devil can threaten—and he might threaten loudly—but with a mind fixed on the truths of who you are and what you have in Christ, you can remain calm, knowing that his threats are empty.

Command authority.

Experts say most of a lion's charges to humans are "mock charges" intended to threaten and incite fear. A proper response to these mock charges is especially vital so they don't turn into attacks. They key here is to command authority and show the lion that you are a threat. The way to do this, experts say, is to clap your hands, shout, and wave your arms. This causes the lion to perceive you as larger than you are and will likely convince it to turn away.[9]

Our victories over Satan happen in a similar way. Though initially you and I might not appear particularly threatening to the devil, we can make some noise to instantly change that! When the devil roars at you, don't flinch or look way. No, stare him in the eye and open your mouth. This is the time to start to make declarations about who you are and what you have in Christ:

- "I am a new person in Christ! Old things have passed away; everything is brand new." (See 2 Corinthians 5:17.)

- "I can do all things through Christ who strengthens me" (Phil. 4:13, NKJV).
- "Jesus took my sin upon himself so that I am made right with God." (See 2 Corinthians 5:21.)

When the devil hears you assert your identity in Christ, He no longer sees only you; He sees Jesus. And if he is smart, he will shut his mouth and retreat.

Stand your ground.

Finally, if the lion proceeds to attack, experts instruct that you should *stay standing*.[10] As we already learned, the lion jumps up to go for your throat or your mouth. If you were to crouch down, he would completely overpower and crush you when he jumped. Though it might seem counter to everything that feels right, standing keeps the lion in full view, which will help you successfully defend yourself if you have to.

The same posture is essential to spiritual victory. Notice how Peter instructed us to deal with the devil.

> Stand firm against him, and be strong in your faith.
> —1 PETER 5:9, NLT

Don't run. Don't cower. *Stand.* This also reflects what we learned in chapter 3 about the purpose of the full armor of God—"to *stand* against the wiles of the devil" (Eph. 6:11).

The way to stand your ground spiritually is simple: don't give up. Your feelings might tell you that you are too exhausted to withstand anything more. They might try to convince you to let up or quit. Don't do it! Remember, the lion doesn't have the stamina to last for too long. When you stand your ground by meditating on God's love and declaring His Word, you will beat the devil down over time. This is ultimate victory!*

---

* Go Beyond the Book: Watch my short teaching titled "Spiritual Warfare: You're Doing It Wrong!" at http://www.kylewinkler.org/videos/spiritual-warfare-youre-doing-it-wrong.

#ActivateTheWord
I am more than a conqueror.

I don't fight for victory, but I stand in the victory of Jesus. His finished work on the cross assures me of forgiveness, healing, peace, provision, protection, and acceptance by God. No attack, threats, lies, or accusations can steal these away from me—not now or in the future. I declare that in Christ I am above the influences of Satan!

18

"I RESIST THE DEVIL"

*Submit yourselves therefore to God. Resist
the devil, and he will flee from you.*

—JAMES 4:7

O NE OF THE first used and most effective weapons in the devil's arsenal against us is *temptation*. Who doesn't know its power? Temptation is a daily visitor that lures us into wanting—craving—something that we shouldn't have. Its bait is a promise of fame, fortune, wisdom, or pleasure. But as we have all learned at some level, temptation never delivers on its promise. Rather, it deceives you and gives you something else. When you eat an extra serving of that delectable dessert, it might satisfy for a minute, but then comes the guilt of ruining your diet. That lustful look that was supposed to be just a momentary escape turns into condemning feelings of dirtiness.

Most often the state you are left in after succumbing to temptation is worse than the state that you were trying to escape. And if you are not careful, the vicious cycle will continue. Satan will offer quick fix after quick fix to move you further and further into his ultimate goal of separating you from God. Thus it is paramount to your destiny that you learn what leads to temptation and how to stand against it, or better yet, how to avoid it from the start.

A Customized Plan of Temptation

Since the Garden of Eden the devil has successfully used temptation on person after person. And after all these years he has honed
his skills on presenting his bait. As we learned in chapter 17, Satan
studies us throughout our lives. By doing so, he is able to create
a customized plan of temptation based on the most effective way
to trip us up and the best time to do so.

The devil knows how to tempt.

Is there a struggle in your life that keeps presenting itself over
and over again? Whatever it is, this is your "signature sin," or
your signature struggle.[1] It is the one dominant, personal weakness that keeps getting you in trouble. By studying your life, the
enemy quickly determines your signature struggle and uses it in
an attempt to lead you into sin.

Consider the first temptation of Adam and Eve. Genesis
records that after Adam was formed, God planted a garden in
Eden where He "made to grow every tree that is pleasant to the
sight and good for food" (Gen. 2:9). God then instructed Adam,
"You may freely eat of every tree of the garden; but of the tree of
the knowledge of good and evil you shall not eat, for in the day
that you eat of it you shall die" (Gen. 2:16–17). God then proceeded to make a partner for Adam. He created animals, birds,
and every other living creature, but nothing was suitable. Finally,
God created the perfect helpmate—a woman named Eve.

Adam had the privilege of seeing God create before His very
own eyes. He is the one who also heard directly from God not to
eat from the tree of the knowledge of good and evil. Eve didn't
have these benefits, which is why I believe she particularly struggled with doubt. Not having heard it directly from God personally, perhaps she doubted His warning to Adam. Or maybe she
even doubted God's goodness and wondered, "Is God trying to
hold something back from us?"

We don't know how long the first couple lived in Eden before the devil's temptation. But even a few days would have been enough time for the devil to recognize Eve's primary struggle and thus concoct a plan that played on it. Consequently, the clever serpent didn't approach Adam, but first approached Eve and asked, "Did God say, 'You shall not eat from any tree in the garden'?" (Gen. 3:1). Satan knew just the weakness to exploit to cause Eve to cave. And it worked.

In the New Testament the devil's plot against Judas is another prime example. When Mary anointed Jesus's feet with expensive perfume, Judas complained, "Why was this perfume not sold for three hundred denarii and the money given to the poor?" (John 12:5). John went on to explain that Judas wasn't really interested in the poor; he was stealing money from the ministry for which he was the treasurer (John 12:6). Here we get a glimpse into what was likely the signature struggle for Judas—the love of money. Unsurprisingly, this is the weakness that Satan used to tempt him. "What will you give me if I betray [Jesus] to you?" Judas asked the chief priests. And with this, he gave up his Savior for thirty pieces of silver (Matt. 26:14–15).

The devil knows when to tempt.

Having the right means of attack is one thing, but knowing the right time to launch it is crucial to its success. The devil isn't likely to make his best attack when you are prepared for him. That would be a waste of his time and energy. Instead, he looks for the moments when your guard is down.

Notice that Satan used this tactic to try to take down Jesus. Jesus's temptation by the devil in the wilderness didn't happen during the first few days but at the end of his time in the wilderness. Matthew records that after fasting for forty days and forty nights, Jesus was famished. At this moment—when Jesus was at His weakest—the devil came with his temptations (Matt. 4:1–3).

If Satan believed he could win in Jesus's moment of weakness, how much more does he believe he can win in yours? This is why Peter instructed that it is imperative to stay alert. You must be aware of the various attacks the enemy uses against you as well as the times that he is likely to launch them. Here are some moments of weakness when the devil is bound to appear.

Stress

Be aware that when the pressure is on, so is Satan. Stress keeps the body and mind in a state of tension and unable to think clearly. In these seasons the devil comes to offer "stress relievers." And while these might seem to ease the pressure for a time, they will be "stress creators" in the long term. Accordingly, medical experts say that stress is one of the greatest influencers of food, drug, alcohol, and tobacco addictions.[2]

Disappointment

Times of disappointment are critical times that make people highly susceptible to the devil's lures. When we are let down from events or situations that hurt us or don't go as planned, the first temptation is to be disappointed or upset with God. Once this happens, almost anything goes. We will take the devil's bait out of sheer rebellion or to fill the void for the "happiness" that we believe we aren't getting.

Anger

Perhaps it is no coincidence that *anger* is just one letter away from *danger*. Paul warned the Ephesians to be especially careful when angry because anger can "make room for the devil" (Eph. 4:27). The danger of anger is that it is a highly emotional state that clouds godly judgment and reason. Instead of acting based on what is right, anger causes us to behave based on what *feels* right at that moment. And what *feels* right when a person is angry is often destructive behavior, including judgment, vindictiveness, violence, or even various means to soothe yourself.

Exhaustion

God designed sleep to be essential for health and well-being. Scientists say that during sleep, our bodies "restore and rejuvenate...grow muscle, repair tissue, and synthesize hormones."[3] Exhaustion from lack of proper sleep and rest has the opposite effects and is known to dramatically impede decision making. This is why the devil almost always brings temptation during times of exhaustion. Sleep deprived minds can't properly process consequences, and sleep deprived bodies don't have the energy to withstand certain offers. We should not be surprised that exhausted people are said to be more likely to abuse drugs and alcohol or to fall into sexual temptation.[4]

How to Resist Temptation

Though temptation may be extremely enticing, falling to it isn't automatic. We can't avoid personal responsibility by claiming, "The devil made me do it!" No, the Bible assures that we are never tempted beyond our abilities to overcome. In fact, it promises that with each temptation, there is a way of escape (1 Cor. 10:13). Yes, God gives us the power to resist every one of Satan's lures and to make him scurry away.

> Submit yourselves therefore to God. Resist the devil, and he will flee from you.
>
> —JAMES 4:7

The Greek word here for *resist* is *anthistēmi*, which means to "stand against" (there is that word *stand* again).[5] This principle is monumental in winning spiritual battles. Just as Jesus experienced in the wilderness, the devil will likely present his temptations more than once. He will try different angles coupled with different tactics to see if they will work against you. But when you maintain your stance against his lures, Satan realizes he is wasting his time, and he decides to move on.

Though Satan may flee, don't ever let down your guard. Luke

added that after Jesus successfully resisted the devil's temptations in the wilderness, the devil "departed from him *until an opportune time*" (Luke 4:13). Yes, the devil always looks for another opportune time to attack—for another moment of weakness. Thus the key to escaping or avoiding Satan's temptations is to live in a constant state of resistance. Here are some certain ways to help you do so.

Guard your mind.

As you have learned by now, the mind is often the first place the devil attacks. This is why it is famously known as "the devil's playground." Because thoughts are forerunners to actions, if Satan can inject wrong thinking, he will eventually trip you up.

Think about it! Junk like depression, fear, and temptation almost always begin in your thoughts. Satan wants nothing more than to use your mind as his garbage dump, where he will drop in thoughts like these: "You will never overcome that," "God doesn't love you," and even, "Just one look, one taste, or one feel won't hurt." When we entertain these thoughts for too long, we eventually act on them.

We all know the power of this:

- When you *think* about your life compared to someone on social media, you start to feel down and then can become depressed.
- When you *think* about an unknown situation, you begin to worry and then become anxious.
- When you start to *think* about an ooey-gooey chocolate something, you start to crave it, and then you devour it.

Where the mind goes, the person follows.

Since the bulk of our spiritual battles begin in the mind, that is where we should begin with our resistance. The first step is to counter the junk Satan attempts to throw into your mind. Practically speaking, this means that when a negative, tempting, or impure thought pops into your mind, you should activate the power of God's Word to counter it. Here's a great truth to declare to help you escape temptation: "I clothe myself in Christ, and I stop thinking about indulging my flesh and its desires." (See Rom. 13:14.)

Second, you resist future thoughts and temptations by proactively guarding your mind with God's Word. This is how the psalmist avoided temptation:

> I have hidden your word in my heart, that I might not sin against you.
> —Psalm 119:11, NLT

The practice of meditating on and declaring God's Word—especially when you are not under any particular temptation—builds up a wall of protection around your mind that impure thoughts cannot easily penetrate. Start by considering your signature struggle and find scriptures that counter it. Keep these running through your mind and mouth at all times.

While it is true that you can't always control the thoughts that enter your mind, you don't have to entertain them, and your life doesn't have to be controlled by them. Satan's influence in your life will diminish when he realizes that your mind is ruled by God's Word and no longer open to his trash.

Watch your step.

The best time to beat temptation isn't during temptation, but before temptation. In other words, if you know that you struggle with a particular issue, then it is wise to avoid whatever or wherever causes it. This is the essence of what Paul wrote to the Ephesians:

> See then that you walk carefully, not as fools, but as wise men, making the most of the time because the days are evil.
> —Ephesians 5:15–16, MEV

Yes, to live in a state of resistance, it is crucial for you to watch your step so that you don't enter places and situations that tend to trigger temptation.

You should also be aware that if the devil can't get you into a place of temptation, he will try to get you close to one. In the Old Testament, this is the trap into which Lot fell. The city of Sodom and Gomorrah was known for its paganism and debauchery. At first, Lot knew better than to live inside of such a place, so he decided to live on the outskirts instead (Gen. 13:12). But living just outside of Sodom kept him within reach of its influence, which eventually lured him in (Gen. 19:1–3).

I have observed that the devil leads people into destruction through three steps. I call these the three Ds of the devil: dabble, deceive, and destroy. When we begin to dabble in unwise situations—especially those that don't initially appear sinful—he then presents arguments as to why we should move in closer. Perhaps this is more influence, more money, more wisdom, or more pleasure. Eventually, like Lot, we are deceived to believe that the end justifies the means, and we move into what will later destroy us. So watch your step. As a wise person said, "He who will play with Satan's bait will quickly be taken by Satan's hook." [6]

Draw near to God.

The bookends that James provided with his instructions to resist the devil are frequently overshadowed by the tremendous promise that the devil will flee. James opened this passage with a charge: "Submit yourselves therefore to God" (James 4:7). And he closed it with something similar: "Draw near to God, and he will draw near to you" (James 4:8). Both the opening and closing affirm the importance of the presence of God as the ultimate means of protection against the devil.

Perhaps there is no better illustration of the protective power of God's presence than David's beloved psalm about the divine shepherd: "Even though I walk through the darkest valley, I fear no evil. For you are with me; your rod and your staff—they comfort me" (Ps. 23:4). When you enter God's presence, you enter the custody of the King of kings. Who or what would dare to come against you here and incite the full force and fury of the Almighty? I love what David says next: "You prepare a table before me in the presence of my enemies" (Ps. 23:5). This image is extraordinary! In God's presence you have the freedom to feast without fear. The enemy may peer in and salivate, but that is all he can do. In God's presence the devil can look, but he can't touch!

I can't stress this enough—time with God is essential for victory in spiritual battles. You can sing every battle hymn of praise, make every declaration of victory, or fast for weeks, but these are all vain repetitions if they are not done out of a life that is grounded in communion with God. After all, it is God's presence that gives any of these actions their power.

Thankfully, spending time with God isn't difficult. Unlike David, you don't have to go to any particular place to draw near to Him. Not a temple. Not even a church building. No, Jesus opened the way for anywhere and anytime access into God's courts. You should enter boldly and frequently! Whenever and wherever you draw near to God, be assured that He draws near to you. And when He is near, you have the full power and protection of His presence, which keeps you ready and able to resist any of Satan's devices.*

#ActivateTheWord
I resist the devil!

I guard my mind with God's Word and I stop thinking about indulging my flesh and its desires. I submit myself to God, I draw near to Him, and I know that He is near to me. Therefore, in the power and protection of God's presence, I stand against temptation, and the devil must flee from me!

---

* Go Beyond the Book: Watch my short teaching titled "The #1 Way to Resist the Devil" at www.kylewinkler.org/videos/the-1-way-to-resist-the-devil.

19

"NO WEAPON FORMED AGAINST ME WILL PROSPER"

No weapon that is fashioned against you
shall prosper, and you shall confute every
tongue that rises against you in judgment.

—ISAIAH 54:17

SATAN LAUNCHES ATTACKS for much more than just the sheer fun of it. Each handcrafted weapon aimed at you is a "smart bomb" zeroed in to succeed in a particular mission.

One of the Bible's greatest promises regarding Satan's attacks comes through the words of the prophet Isaiah: "No weapon that is fashioned against you shall prosper.... This is the heritage of the servants of the LORD" (Isa. 54:17). While it is certainly a comforting word, many question its reality. The devil's weapons appear to achieve their mission all the time. People lose their jobs, their health, and their loved ones. Disasters destroy homes and neighborhoods. And the list goes on. Certainly plenty of bad things happen to God's servants every day. I am sure you can name some attacks that seem to have succeeded in your life.

So what do we make of God's promise? Has He forgotten or reconsidered? Absolutely not! God's Word is His bond. In fact, He has already made good on His promise. As we will explore here, the key to its realization in our lives is first to know what the ultimate mission of Satan's attacks is and to stand on what God already did to abort that mission.

The Ultimate Mission of an Attack

You must understand that an attack is a means but not an end. In other words, financial struggles, health problems, and disasters, for example, are merely the weapons Satan uses to accomplish a goal that is even greater than stealing from you or causing you pain.

Consider the infamous attacks on Job. The Bible records that he was a man whom God called righteous—"one who feared God and turned away from evil" (Job 1:1). One day, after observing Job, Satan barged into God's courts to insist that Job's fear of the Lord wasn't genuine. He believed that Job loved God only because he was blessed and protected by Him. Satan contended that if God's blessing and protection were taken away, Job would reconsider God's goodness and curse Him to His face (Job 1:8–11). So Satan proceeded to test his theory with attacks from every angle. He took away Job's possessions, family, and health.

You might think that the extreme physical, mental, and emotional anguish Job endured because of these attacks was enough to satisfy Satan. But these attacks were not designed only to harm Job. No, as we see from the earlier conversation between him and God, ultimately Satan used these attacks as a means to get Job to question God's goodness. In the New Testament Paul indicated something similar. He revealed that attacks are meant to keep us from knowing that God is for us and that He loves us (Rom. 8:31–35). In other words, the ultimate mission of an attack isn't only pain, but to put God's good character in question to cause distance and separation from Him.

Think about the attacks you have faced. Don't they almost always incite questions that try to make you doubt God? When our health is under siege, many are tempted to believe it is the result of God's punishment. "Is God mad at me?" one might question. If finances are stricken, God's faithfulness comes into question.

"Does He really care for me?" one might ask. Given enough time, each of these weapons matures into provoking a total distrust of God. This is a slippery slope where doubts or questions become definitive declarations, such as "God doesn't love me" or "God has abandoned me."

If the devil can bring you to the point of eroding your confidence in God, then he ultimately traps you in despair. After all, if you can't trust God, then who can you trust? Nothing is more hopeless! In this place many destructive decisions are made, which only perpetuate feelings of separation. Of course, nothing could be further from the truth. God never moves; He remains as close as ever. Still, for many perception is reality. And the devil achieves his mission.

The Assignment of an Accusation

The Bible gives two job descriptions of Satan: adversary and accuser (1 Pet. 5:8; Rev. 12:10). Many of the attacks mentioned so far fall under his role of adversary. But it is his role as an accuser that is especially effective at achieving his goal. With accusations he attempts to hold you in separation from God through guilt, shame, and condemnation. At this point he changes your concept of who God is based on who you are and what you have done. To do this, he whispers lies such as "You are too dirty—God *can't* love you," and provokes fear with "Because you have failed, God will punish you."

I well know the destructive power of Satan's accusations, for accusation is the weapon he used to try to shut me down at the very beginning of my ministry. Literally within months of stepping out, I was bombarded with threats about insecurities, weaknesses, and sins dating all the way back to potty training![1] The devil's accusations provided the evidence to back up why I would never be good enough or why I was too messed up to be used by God. I started to believe that he was right, and I considered quitting ministry to do something else.

About a week into this warfare, when I was beat to tears, I

heard the Lord speak to me. "You stand at a crossroads," God said. "You can go to the noose or to the nails—to be hung or to be held." It was a curious word, but then the Lord began to reveal its full meaning. He showed me the effects of Satan's accusations on Judas, the disciple who betrayed Jesus. I saw that it wasn't so much the horrible sin of betraying Jesus, but the follow-up accusations that overwhelmed Judas with so much shame that he ran to a noose to hang himself. This was the road down which Satan intended to lead me. As he did Judas, Satan sought to hang me with accusations.

The other direction from this crossroads was the way to the nails—to be held. That is when God directed me to the Via Dolorosa, which is the historical road that Jesus traveled on His way to the cross. Suddenly there I was at the end of this road. With my mind's eye I saw myself standing at the foot of the cross, looking up at Jesus, who was covered in the ugliness of my sin and shame.

As I peered deep into Jesus's wounds, I began to grasp the extent to which He went to destroy the works of the enemy in my life. I saw how the nails of crucifixion laid to waste every weapon Satan had formed against me. Every sin from my past, every word spoken against me, every insecurity, and every lie was intercepted and canceled before it could achieve its mission. Seeing the cross left no question about God's goodness and His love for me; it dramatically proved just how wide, how long, how high, and how deep His love really is (Eph. 3:18).

After I spent some time in reflection and repentance, the Lord asked me to list each accusation hanging over my head. When I was finished with this painful undertaking, He instructed me to cover the list with the word *blood* and with drawings of a cross. Though excruciating, I followed God's directions until I could no longer make out the accusations I had itemized underneath. Then God said, "Rip that paper to shreds!"

What happened next was revolutionary. With my list obliterated, I was reminded of what Paul wrote to the Colossians:

> You who were dead in your trespasses…God made alive together with him, having forgiven us all our trespasses, by canceling the record of debt that stood against us with its legal demands. This he set aside, nailing it to the cross.
> —COLOSSIANS 2:13–14, ESV

The legal demands of a debt of sin is separation from God. And the list that God instructed me to create represented this record filled with everything Satan used to accomplish his mission. By asking me to shred this paper, God wanted me to freshly see the power of the cross to abort the assignment of Satan's weapons. In this moment, when I understood the enormity of what had happened, I heard Jesus's final words on the cross declared personally over me. "It is finished," He assured (John 19:30).

This was a life-changing encounter through which God revealed how I am held. The finished work of the nails of Jesus's crucifixion was meant to hold me in an assurance of righteousness not based on who I am and what I have done but on who He is and what He has done.

Your Part in God's Promise

If you study God's promises, you will notice that they are often coupled with two parts: God's part and our part. God's promise to thwart the success of Satan's weapons is no exception. To see this, look at the breakdown of Isaiah 54:17 (NLT):

- *God's promise:* "No weapon turned against you will succeed."
- *Our part:* "You will silence every voice raised up to accuse you."
- *God's part:* "Their vindication [righteousness] will come from me."

As God revealed to me, the cross was His once-and-for-all solution to destroy the works of the enemy. There is nothing more for God to do. Some two thousand years ago He made good on His part of the promise through the righteousness given to us by Jesus's shed blood.

Our part to ensure that Satan's weapons don't succeed is to silence his accusations. We do this with a counterattack based on two surefire weapons of righteousness:

> They have conquered [the accuser] by the blood of the Lamb and by the word of their testimony.
>
> —Revelation 12:11

Yes, we completely demolish the power of Satan's accusations by the blood of Jesus and the word of our testimonies. Let's now look at how to practically apply these two weapons.

"By the blood of the Lamb"

When I so intimately saw the magnitude of what Jesus did on the cross, I was led to repentance. This is exactly what Paul indicated that Jesus's taking our punishment is supposed to do.

> Do you not realize that God's kindness is meant to lead you to repentance?
>
> —Romans 2:4

Unfortunately, for many today repentance is a foreign concept. Yet it is the way we conquer Satan's accusations using "the blood of the Lamb." Allow me to explain.

Throughout the New Testament, the Greek word for *repent* is *metanoeō*, which simply means to "change one's mind." [2] According to the *Dictionary of Biblical Languages*, repentance leads to a changed life based on two mind changes: one concerning sin and one concerning righteousness. [3] Too often people teach about only one of these changes and not the other. But that is a mistake. As we will see, both are crucial to accomplishing real transformation.

Change your mind concerning sin.

As we go throughout our Christian lives, it is easy to become calloused to the effects of sin. If we aren't careful, we can slowly slip into destructive lifestyle patterns by believing, "God doesn't mind; I will just ask for forgiveness later."

The power of a fresh look at the cross is that it reminds you of just how terrible sin really is (Rom. 7:13). In the moment that I truly saw the mutilation that my sin and shame caused Jesus, I fell to my knees, wept, and immediately apologized to God for the ways I had hurt Him.

If you feel bombarded by accusations, I emphatically encourage you to take them all to the cross—right now. If you have sin in your life, confess it there and freshly apply the blood that Jesus shed so long ago to cleanse your sin today. Make this declaration: "I take my sin and shame to the cross, and I receive the forgiveness that Jesus's blood provided for me" (1 John 1:9).

Sometimes the enemy brings up sins that you already confessed. He wants to invalidate the power of the cross to make you believe that they were never really forgiven. To be sure, you don't need to confess these sins all over again. You simply need to remember the cross in order to change your mind concerning their power over you. Let's look at this now.

Change your mind concerning righteousness.

Confession of sin is vital, but once you do this, God doesn't desire for you to stay in sorrow. The second part of repentance is that God wants you to renew your mind: by Jesus's blood, you are made righteous.

A fresh look at the cross is an opportunity to do as Paul instructed: clothe yourself in Christ (Rom. 13:14). God doesn't want you to continue to see yourself as filthy and sin-stained. No, He desires for you to see yourself covered in the clothing of

Jesus—blood-stained and holy! You have nothing to grieve. In Christ you are clean, pure, spotless, and white. Yes, you get to look like Jesus because you are covered in Jesus! Make this declaration: "I clothe myself in Christ. I am no longer identified by sin and shame, but by the righteous identity of Jesus."

To silence Satan, it is crucial that you change your mind concerning your standing before God. In Christ you have a blameless identity that the devil can't accuse: you are loved, you are accepted, and you are made new. Yes, you are brought near to God by the blood of Christ (Eph. 2:13). This is amazing! The plot of the enemy is made powerless because the plan of the cross has made you righteous.

"By the word of their testimony"

The Bible assures that we conquer the accuser by the word of our testimony (Rev. 12:11). To put it simply: your testimony is the evidence of the Lord's work in your life. Some people have dramatic stories about overcoming lifestyles of addiction, abuse, or promiscuity. Others have inspiring stories about how God's grace helped them to live purely since their youth. Our stories are all different, but they are all equally important.

Giving your testimony is tremendously powerful way to have an impact on both yourself and others. Recounting your testimony reminds you of God's goodness in your past, which helps you remain confident in His goodness for your future. Sharing your testimony with others builds faith and expectancy that what God did for you, He will also do for them.

The devil is acutely aware of the power of testimony, which is why he works vehemently to keep your story from being told. Remember the illustration from chapter 17, about how a lion goes for the kill? A lion attacks the throat or covers the mouth of his prey to suffocate it. Satan uses accusations for this same goal. If he can convince you that your past is beyond the forgiveness of

God, he silences you with the belief that you are not qualified enough to be used by God.

As we have learned, the power of the cross canceled the evidence that stood against you. There is nothing for Satan to hold over your head. When you share your testimony, you stand on the truth of your righteousness in Christ. And thus you alert the devil that his accusations are dead to you; his mission is aborted!*

#ActivateTheWord

No weapon formed against me will prosper.

At the cross Jesus canceled the record of my wrongs so that I am forgiven and declared righteous. There is nothing for the devil to hold over my head. I silence Satan's threats and accusations by the blood of the Lamb and the word of my testimony. I won't let up, give up, back up, or shut up!

---

* Go Beyond the Book: Watch my short teaching titled "How to Intercept Satan's Weapons" at www.kylewinkler.org/videos/how-to-intercept-satans-weapons.

20

"IT IS FINISHED"

[Jesus] said, "It is finished." Then
he bowed his head and gave up his spirit.

—JOHN 19:30

So FAR WE have explored many life-transforming declarations. But I have saved one for last—one I consider the most powerful of all. In fact, it is the declaration that Jesus saved for last too.

In the world's darkest hour—at the height of sin's ugliest achievement, when Jesus's body was utterly shredded on the cross—Jesus amazingly mustered up the energy to make one last announcement: "It is finished." Then only a few seconds later He bowed His head to die (John 19:30).

I imagine that to most of the onlookers on crucifixion day, Jesus's declaration must have sounded like the last desperate words of a madman. "Sure, it's finished!" they likely mocked. "The 'king of the Jews' has reached His crowning moment—death on a cross." Oh, but little did they know! "It is finished" wasn't the gasp of a life about to be extinguished. This was certainly no declaration of defeat, but one of a mighty, mighty victory! And from that day forward, these final words from the cross would serve to change history.

A Mission Accomplished

The cross wasn't the only instance in which Jesus spoke of a finished work. Just before His betrayal and arrest, He prayed to His

Father: "I glorified you on earth by finishing the work that you gave me to do" (John 17:4). The Greek word used here for *finish* is *teleō*. And it means what you would expect—"to complete" or "to fulfill." [1] The context in which Jesus uses it, however, is a telling clue that there was much more to His time on earth than what meets the eye. It is the hint of a surprise soon to be revealed.

And so it was. Bursting forth atop Calvary's hill, Jesus's final declaration lit up the sky like a fireworks grand finale.

> When Jesus had received the wine, he said, "*It is finished.*" Then he bowed his head and gave up his spirit.
>
> —JOHN 19:30

Here, at the climax of His crucifixion, the word for *finished* changed from *teleō* to *tetelestai*—a highly unique form of *teleō* that was never used in the New Testament before or after the cross. While our English translation doesn't convey this, the difference between these two words for *finished* is profoundly revealing. The original word means "to complete" while the declaration on the cross means "mission accomplished!" Accordingly, "It is finished" was as if a curtain lifted to make a grand reveal. In the foresight of the cross Jesus hinted at something about to be finished. But on the cross He revealed, "Mission accomplished! Everything that had to be done has been done! It is finished!" [2]

Jesus's declaration begs the question: "What was this grand accomplishment?" I'm glad you asked! The Bible makes it crystal clear:

> The Son of God was revealed for this purpose, to destroy the works of the devil.
>
> —1 JOHN 3:8

How awesome! "It is finished" was Jesus's declaration that the works of Satan were destroyed—the devil's devices demolished, his plot aborted, and his power stripped away. This deserves some serious praise!

How the Mission Was Accomplished

As we have already discussed, the original creation is indicative of God's perfect will. Adam and Eve enjoyed a flawless creation, intimacy with the Father, righteousness, knowledge only of godly ways, and a life free of sickness and death. At the end of His work, God proclaimed, "It was very good," for good reason—evil was nowhere to be found (Gen. 1:31).

In a risky move God gave control of His freshly created earth to a new owner—humankind. Adam, Eve, and their offspring (us!) were to manage and be in authority over "every living thing that moves" (Gen. 1:28). This was something Satan believed he could exploit. After he was kicked out of heaven because he couldn't be God, the devil devised a plan to steal authority from humankind to become the god of earth (John 14:30). And as the story goes, that is precisely what happened.

When the first couple gave in to Satan's temptation in the garden, they essentially handed over control, and the works of the devil were instantly apparent. Adam and Eve were no longer innocent; they became aware of their guilt and shame. Suddenly the soil became difficult to work and getting food became a struggle. Death, sickness, and disease began to reign (Rom. 5:12). And the saddest outcome was that God could no longer be in intimate relationship with the people He loved so much. Offerings, sacrifices, and laws were later instituted to make restitution for all of this sin. But they didn't work. No, to finally rescue His creation and His people, God had a greater plan in store.

Jesus is the personification of God's ultimate plan. He entered this sin-wrecked world and focused His time here on overthrowing Satan's reign in order to restore creation to the way it was before the devil wrecked it.

It is amazing to understand how everything about Jesus's life, death, and resurrection accomplished this mission. Let's explore this now.

Health and authority restored

Peter summarized Jesus's ministry by noting that He "went about doing good and healing all who were oppressed by the devil" (Acts 10:38). Jesus's healings and exorcisms were a type of victory over Satan. As we explored in chapter 16, Jesus's healings demonstrated that divine health had returned. His exorcisms demonstrated the return of authority. Amazingly, He gave the power of His name and His Word to activate both healing and authority to all God's people. "By using my name they will cast out demons...they will lay their hands on the sick, and they will recover," He assured (Mark 16:17–18).

The mind restored

In God's original creation, humankind had no knowledge of evil. Thus evil thoughts, speech, and actions had no influence. With Adam and Eve's fall, however, this immediately changed, and the Bible records that their eyes were opened (Gen. 3:7). With this God declared, "The man has become like one of us, knowing good and evil" (Gen. 3:22). Jesus's teaching ministry was strategically aimed at defeating the knowledge of evil. Because of it, we have His Word to renew our minds with the knowledge of good and be transformed into the mind of Christ (Rom. 12:2).

Relationship and righteousness restored

The prophet Isaiah prophesied that Jesus would be "despised and rejected by others; a man of suffering" (Isa. 53:3). He then concluded, "Yet he bore the sin of many, and made intercession for the transgressors" (Isa. 53:12). Jesus's crucifixion fulfilled this prophecy that through His sacrifice humanity would be rescued and redeemed. Allow me to explain.

First, *as a sacrifice* Jesus paid the penalty of death that humankind deserves because of their sin. This is what Hebrews boasts: "He...put away sin by the sacrifice of himself" (Heb. 9:26, ESV). Second, *through His sacrifice* He took our identity of sin and gave us His identity of righteousness (2 Cor. 5:21). In doing so, He overcame our separation from God. Now covered in the holiness of Christ, we are restored into relationship with God and may boldly enter His presence. Finally, Mark asserted that Jesus gave His life as "a ransom for many" (Mark 10:45). This is marvelous! *Because of Jesus's sacrifice* we are freed from bondage to sin and to Satan's rule.

Do you see everything that Jesus's sacrifice accomplished? We are purified, made righteous, restored to relationship with God, cleansed from sin, and empowered to overcome the devil. These are all the astonishing results of Christ's victory over the works of Satan—and they all were accomplished on the cross.

Eternal life restored

As we have seen, by the time Jesus declared, "It is finished," He had already accomplished awesome victory over Satan. But there was more to come. Therefore, Jesus's declaration is also a prophetic one. You see, on the cross Jesus had yet to complete the validation of His mission, which was to rise from the dead. Resurrection was absolutely paramount to prove everything else He accomplished. Without rising from the dead, all His work before would have been for nothing.

Prophetically, when Jesus declared, "It is finished," He alerted the devil that nothing could keep Him down—a resurrection was coming. And indeed it did! Paul boasted that Jesus "was declared to be Son of God with power according to the spirit of holiness by resurrection from the dead" (Rom. 1:4). Yes, through His life, death, and resurrection, Jesus triumphed over every force that opposed Him and conquered the final work of the devil, which is death. "Death has been swallowed up in victory," Paul proclaimed (1 Cor. 15:54). With this, Jesus therefore restored God's perfect will for His people to enjoy eternal life in His presence.

The following chart summarizes the amazing ways Jesus accomplished His mission of overcoming the works of Satan in our lives.

God's Perfect Will	Satan's Work	Because of Jesus's Victory
Divine health	Sickness and disease	Access to healing in Jesus's name
Dominion for humanity	Stolen authority	Authority over Satan in Jesus's name
Knowledge of godly ways	Knowledge of evil	The transformation of the mind by God's Word; the mind of Christ
Righteousness and relationship with God	Sin and separation from God	Relationship with God based on Christ's righteousness
Eternal life in God's presence	Death	Eternal life in God's presence

Fascinatingly, the devil didn't see any of this coming. In fact, when Jesus was on the cross, Satan thought he had won the victory. Shortly before Jesus's final declaration, He cried out, "My God, my God, why have you forsaken me?" (Matt. 27:46). With this, Satan and his minions must have had a victory dance, celebrating that they had achieved their mission to separate the Father from the Son. But their party was short lived. Just moments later, when Jesus declared *tetelestai*—"It is finished"—the devil knew that the tables had been turned. And certainly they were!

The cross was never something that unfortunately *happened* to Jesus. No, the cross was always the plan of the Father and the Son from before creation (1 Pet. 1:20). For a while Jesus allowed the devil to believe that he had led Him to the cross. But Jesus went to the cross voluntarily! All the while He was actually leading Satan into a trap through which He accomplished His mission to destroy the works of the devil. The cross was the ultimate "gotcha!"

In the most stunning way, "It is finished" uncovered the most brilliant strategy in history. The Bible reveals that if Satan and his forces would have truly understood the plan of the cross, "they would not have crucified the Lord of glory" (1 Cor. 2:8). But by that time Satan had lost, and there was nothing he could do to escape that truth.

Whatever It Is... It Is Finished!

Shortly after my encounter at the cross, God instructed me to make the cross a central theme in my ministry. That is why so much of what you have read throughout this book is in some way rooted in it. But in addition to teaching about the cross, God charged me to impart its power into those to whom I minister.

When I preach, I do this in several ways, depending on the situation. Sometimes I lead the congregation into declarations regarding everything received because of Christ's finished work: healing, deliverance, righteousness, and so on. Then we close with a powerful shout of victory: "It is finished!" Other times I lay hands on individuals and directly declare, "It is finished!" over them. Whatever the format I use, the power of the cross is always sure to bring a freedom and victory that many have never experienced.

The great news is that you can experience this power for yourself right now. As we reviewed at the beginning of this book, God's spoken Word succeeds in whatever it is meant to do. And "It is finished" was meant to announce the defeat of the devil. As you declare it out of your mouth, I believe it will go to work to accomplish its mission in every area of your life.

Remember, Jesus made His declaration at the most painful time, when He was just one breath away from death. The timing of His declaration reveals that even in the most challenging and darkest circumstances—when you feel cut to the core, when everyone is against you, when it looks as if all is lost—you can still make a declaration of victory. In fact, in these moments it is crucial that you do.

Declaring, "It is finished," over your life or situation alerts the devil that you are standing firm on God's Word about who you are and what you have in Christ. It forewarns Satan that your current circumstances are not the final answer—they will not kill you. Instead, something good is about to happen. Yes, a resurrection is on the way! Over whatever situation you are in, activate the power of God's Word: "It is finished!" *

#ActivateTheWord
It is finished!

The life, death, and resurrection of Jesus have completely destroyed the works of the devil in my life. Guilt and shame are finished; sickness is finished; fear and insecurity are finished. I am no longer in bondage to sin, and the victory of Jesus's finished work has freed me to enjoy a new life in the glory of God's presence—forever.

---

* Go Beyond the Book: Watch my short teaching titled "Whatever It Is...It Is Finished!" at www.kylewinkler.org/videos/whatever-it-is-it-is-finished.

NOTES

CHAPTER 1: THE POWER OF ONE SPOKEN SENTENCE

1. A. W. Tozer, *The Pursuit of God* (Camp Hill, PA: Christian Publications, 1982), 73.

2. James Strong, *Strong's Exhaustive Concordance* (Nashville: Thomas Nelson, 2010), Hebrew and Aramaic Dictionary, no. 922 and no. 8414.

3. "The Names of God in the Old Testament," Blue Letter Bible, accessed August 5, 2016, https://www.blueletterbible.org/study/misc/name_god.cfm.

4. Walter A. Elwell and Barry J. Beitzel, *Baker Encyclopedia of the Bible* (Grand Rapids: Baker, 1988).

5. Adapted from "Scientists Baffled by Laws of Nature," Every Student, accessed August 5, 2016, www.everystudent.com/wires/organized.html. Used with permission.

6. James Trefil, *Reading the Mind of God* (New York: Anchor, 1989), 1.

7. "Scientists Baffled by Laws of Nature."

8. Ibid.

9. Ibid.

10. Mark Pretorius, "Sound: Conceivably the Creative Language of God, Holding All of Creation in Concert," *Verbum et Ecclesia* 32, no. 1, November 3, 2011, www.ve.org.za/index.php/VE/article/view/485/851.

11. "So What Is String Theory, Then?" SuperstringTheory.com, accessed August 5, 2016, www.superstringtheory.com/basics/basic4.html.

12. Pretorius, "Sound."

13. Ibid.

14.   Online Etymology Dictionary, s.v. "universe," accessed October 31, 2016, www.etymonline.com/index.php?term =universe&allowed_in_frame=0; idem, s.v. "verse," accessed October 31, 2016, www.etymonline.com/index.php?term=verse.

15.   Chris Woodford, "Sound," Explain That Stuff, updated June 21, 2016, accessed August 5, 2016, www.explainthatstuff.com/sound .html.

16.   Tozer, *Pursuit of God*, 75.

CHAPTER 2: THE BIBLICAL PRINCIPLE OF SPEAKING SCRIPTURE

1.   Billy Graham, *Where I Am: Heaven, Eternity, and Our Life Beyond* (Nashville: W Publishing, 2015), 237.

2.   Jennifer Speake, ed., *Oxford Dictionary of Proverbs* (Oxford: Oxford University Press, 2015), 93.

3.   Lexicon: Strong's H1696—*dabar*, Blue Letter Bible, accessed November 17, 2016, https://www.blueletterbible.org/lang/lexicon /lexicon.cfm?Strongs=H1696&t=KJV.

4.   J. W. L. Hoad, "Promise," ed. D. R. W. Wood, I. H. Marshall, A. R. Millard, J. I. Packer, and D. J. Wiseman, *New Bible Dictionary* (Leicester, UK; Downers Grove, IL: InterVarsity, 1996).

5.   *New Oxford American Dictionary*, s.v. "authority" (New York: Oxford University Press, 2013).

6.   Tom Brown, "Releasing Your Angels to Work for You," Tom Brown Ministries, accessed August 8, 2016, tbm.org/releasin.htm.

7.   "Meditate," Eugene E. Carpenter and Philip W. Comfort, *Holman Treasury of Key Bible Words: 200 Greek and 200 Hebrew Words Defined and Explained* (Nashville: Broadman & Holman, 2000), 123.

CHAPTER 3: HOW TO PUT THE WORD TO WORK FOR YOU

1.   C. H. Spurgeon, *According to Promise* (New York: Funk & Wagnalls, 1887), 61.

2.   Linda Long, in discussion with the author, e-mail, July 19, 2013. Used by permission. See godscureforanxiety.com for more information.

3.   James Strong, *Strong's Exhaustive Concordance* (Nashville: Thomas Nelson, 2010), Greek Dictionary of the New Testament, 3053.

4.   See the chapter "The Uniform of the Righteous" in Kyle Winkler, *Silence Satan: Shutting Down the Enemy's Attacks, Threats, Lies, and Accusations* (Lake Mary, FL: Charisma House, 2014).

5. "How Can Jesus and the Bible Both Be the Word of God?" Got Questions?, accessed August 8, 2016, www.gotquestions.org/Jesus -Bible-Word-God.html.

6. Lexicon: Strong's G4487—*rhēma*, Blue Letter Bible, accessed November 16, 2016, https://www.blueletterbible.org/lang/lexicon /lexicon.cfm?Strongs=G4487&t=KJV.

Chapter 4: You Are What You Speak

1. "This Year's Top New Year's Resolution? Fitness!!," Nielsen, January 8, 2015, accessed August 8, 2016, www.nielsen.com/us/en /insights/news/2015/2015s-top-new-years-resolution-fitness.html.

2. Geza Vermes, *Jesus the Jew: A Historian's Reading of the Gospels* (Minneapolis: Fortress, 1981), 92.

3. The source of this quote cannot be verified. It has been attributed to many people throughout history.

4. The source of this quote cannot be verified. It has been attributed to many people throughout history.

Chapter 5: "God Chose Me"

1. Dawn Davenport, "23 Crucial Questions to Ask When Adopting from Foster Care," Creating a Family, February 9, 2015, accessed August 9, 2016, https://creatingafamily.org/adoption -category/23-crucial-questions-you-must-ask-when-adopting-from -foster-care/.

2. Ibid.

3. Walter A. Elwell and Barry J. Beitzel, "Abraham," in *Baker Encyclopedia of the Bible*, ed. Walter A. Elwell (Grand Rapids, MI: Baker, 1988), 1.

Chapter 6: "I Am Loved Unconditionally"

1. Thomas F. Torrance, *Karl Barth: An Introduction to Early Theology* (New York: T&T Clark, 1962), 7.

2. Ronnie McBrayer, "Jesus Loves Me This I Know…," Beliefnet, accessed August 9, 2016, www.beliefnet.com/columnists /leavingsalem/2012/06/jesus-loves-me-this-i-know.html.

3. Ibid.

4. Paul Froese and Christopher Bader, *America's Four Gods: What We Say About God—and What That Says about Us* (New York: Oxford University Press, 2010), 15–36.

5. Ibid.

6. Ibid.

7. Ibid.

8. Gerald H. Wilson, "The Structure of the Psalter," in *Interpreting the Psalms: Issues and Approaches*, ed. David Firth and Philip S. Johnston (Downers Grove, IL: InterVarsity, 2005), 229.

9. *Merriam-Webster Online*, s.v. "love," accessed August 9, 2016, www.merriam-webster.com/dictionary/love.

10. Lexicon: Strong's G2889—*kosmos*, Blue Letter Bible, accessed November 16, 2016, https://www.blueletterbible.org/lang/lexicon/lexicon.cfm?Strongs=G2889&t=KJV.

CHAPTER 7: "I AM A NEW PERSON IN CHRIST"

1. *New Oxford American Dictionary*, s.v. "metamorphosis" (New York: Oxford University Press, 2013).

2. "Metamorphosis," Butterfly School, accessed August 9, 2016, www.butterflyschool.org/new/meta.html.

3. Ibid.

4. Ibid.

CHAPTER 8: "GOD HAS GREAT PLANS FOR ME"

1. "Major Depression Facts," Clinical-depression.co.uk, accessed August 9, 2016, www.clinical-depression.co.uk/dlp/depression-information/major-depression-facts/; Edward Shorter, "Sad, Worthless, Hopeless?" *Psychology Today*, June 21, 2014, accessed August 9, 2016, https://www.psychologytoday.com/blog/how-everyone-became-depressed/201406/sad-worthless-hopeless.

2. R. Morgan Griffin, "Lifestyle Tips for Treatment-Resistant Depression: How You Live Can Help Support Expert Medical Care," WebMD, April 29, 2011, accessed October 31, 2016, www.webmd.com/depression/features/lifestyle-tips-for-treatment-resistant-depression#1.

CHAPTER 9: "I DON'T WORRY ABOUT ANYTHING"

1. "Worry, Anxiety, Fear, or Panic," Psychology Solution, accessed August 10, 2016, www.psychology-solution.com/anxiety/worry-anxiety-fear-panic.

2. *New Oxford American Dictionary*, s.v. "faith" (New York: Oxford University Press, 2013).

3. "Mark Twain: Quotes," Goodreads, accessed October 31, 2016, www.goodreads.com/quotes/31860-i-ve-lived-through-some-terrible-things-in-my-life-some.

4.   Don Joseph Goewey, "85 Percent of What We Worry About Never Happens," Huffington Post, August 25, 2015, accessed August 10, 2016, www.huffingtonpost.com/don-joseph-goewey-/85-of-what -we-worry-about_b_8028368.html.

5.   "Fun BrainTeasers and Riddles for Kids," No Bullying, updated April 16, 2015, accessed October 10, 2016, https://nobullying .com/riddles-for-kids/.

6.   *New Oxford American Dictionary*, s.v. "be" (New York: Oxford University Press, 2013).

CHAPTER 10: "I ENJOY MY LIFE"

1.   "Alice Morse Earle: Quotes," Goodreads, accessed August 11, 2016, https://www.goodreads.com/author/quotes/44874.Alice_Morse _Earle.

2.   Linda Sapadin, "Fear of Missing Out," PsychCentral, accessed August 11, 2016, psychcentral.com/blog/archives/2015/10/12 /fear-of-missing-out/.

3.   Elizabeth Cohen, "Blaming Others Can Ruin Your Health," CNN, August 18, 2011, accessed August 11, 2016, www.cnn.com /2011/HEALTH/08/17/bitter.resentful.ep/.

CHAPTER 11: "THE JOY OF THE LORD IS MY STRENGTH"

1.   *New Oxford American Dictionary*, s.v. "disappointment" (New York: Oxford University Press, 2013).

2.   *New Oxford American Dictionary*, s.v. "happy" (New York: Oxford University Press, 2013).

3.   Ed Diener, Richard E Lucas, and Shigehiro Oishi, "Subjective Well-Being," in *Handbook of Positive Psychology*, ed. C.R. Snyder and Shane J. Lopez (New York: Oxford University Press, 2002), 66–67.

CHAPTER 12: "SOMETHING GOOD WILL HAPPEN TO ME"

1.   Matthew Henry, *Matthew Henry's Commentary on the Whole Bible: Complete and Unabridged in One Volume* (Peabody, MA: Hendrickson, 1994), 778.

2.   Jerry Bridges, "Praying in Faith," Billy Graham Evangelistic Association, March 28, 2013, accessed August 15, 2016, billygraham .org/decision-magazine/march-2013/praying-in-faith/.

Chapter 13: "I Can Do Whatever God Wants Me to Do"

1.   I. Howard Marshall and David Peterson, eds., *Witness to the Gospel: The Theology of Acts* (Grand Rapids: Eerdmans, 1998), 230–31.

Chapter 14: "God Is My Vindicator"

1.   *New Oxford American Dictionary*, s.v. "vindicate" (New York: Oxford University Press, 2013).

Chapter 15: "God Provides for All My Needs"

1.   Darren E. Grem, *The Blessings of Business: How Corporations Shaped Conservative Christianity* (New York: Oxford University Press, 2016), 2.

2.   "Faith Channels for Everyone," TBN Networks, accessed October 31, 2016, https://www.tbn.org/about/images/TBN_Networks _info.pdf.

3.   Lilly Family School of Philanthropy, Giving USA 2016, Giving USA Foundation.

Chapter 16: "I Am Healed"

1.   Lexicon: Strong's G7495—*rapha'*, Blue Letter Bible, accessed November 16, 2016, https://www.blueletterbible.org/lang/lexicon /lexicon.cfm?Strongs=H7495&t=KJV.

Chapter 17: "I Am More Than a Conqueror"

1.   "Lion," Speed of Animals, accessed August 18, 2016, www .speedofanimals.com/animals/lion.

2.   "Predatory Behaviour," Lion Alert, accessed August 18, 2016, https://lionalert.org/page/predatory-behaviour.

3.   Encyclopedia.com, s.v. "tribulation," accessed November 17, 2016, www.encyclopedia.com/humanities/dictionaries-thesauruses -pictures-and-press-releases/tribulation.

4.   Bible Hub, *Strong's Concordance*, Greek 5228, *huper*, accessed November 17, 2016, biblehub.com/greek/5228.htm.

5.   Lexicon: Strong's G3528—*nikaō*, Blue Letter Bible, accessed November 17, 2016, https://www.blueletterbible.org/lang/lexicon /lexicon.cfm?t=nasb&strongs=g3528.

6.   Lexicon: Strong's G5245—*hypernikaō*, accessed November 16, 2016, https://www.blueletterbible.org/lang/lexicon/lexicon.cfm ?Strongs=G5245&t=KJV.

7.   "Never Forget That You Are More Than a Conqueror," Renner, January 20, 2016, accessed August 18, 2016, www.renner.org /victorious-living/never-forget-you-are-more-than-a-conqueror/.

8.   John Coppinger, "How to Survive a Lion Attack," Discover Wildlife, July 22, 2010, accessed August 8, 2016, www .discoverwildlife.com/travel/how-survive-lion-attack.

9.   Ibid.

10.   Ibid.

CHAPTER 18: "I RESIST THE DEVIL"

1.   Michael Smalley, "Discovering Your Signature Sin," Smalley Institute, January 14, 2007, accessed August 22, 2016, www.smalley .cc/discovering-your-signature-sin/.

2.   "Stress Symptoms: Effects on Your Body and Behavior," Mayo Clinic, April 28, 2016, www.mayoclinic.org/healthy-lifestyle/stress -management/in-depth/stress-symptoms/art-20050987.

3.   "Excessive Sleepiness: Why Do We Need Sleep?" Sleep Foundation, accessed August 22, 2016, https://sleepfoundation.org /excessivesleepiness/content/why-do-we-need-sleep.

4.   "Why Sleep Is Important," American Psychological Association, accessed August 22, 2016, www.apa.org/topics/sleep /why.aspx; Linda Richter, "Sleep-Deprived Teens Are at Increased Risk of Substance Abuse," National Center on Addiction and Substance Abuse, December 9, 2014, accessed August 22, 2016, www .centeronaddiction.org/the-buzz-blog/sleep-deprived-teens-are-increased-risk-substance-use.

5.   James Swanson, *Dictionary of Biblical Languages with Semantic Domains: Greek (New Testament)* (Oak Harbor: Logos Research Systems, 1997).

6.   Thomas Brooks, *Precious Remedies Against Satan's Devices: Being a Companion for Christians of All Denominations* (Philadelphia: Jonathan Pounder, 1810), 312.

CHAPTER 19: "NO WEAPON FORMED AGAINST ME WILL PROSPER"

1.   See the chapter "The Noose or the Nails" in Kyle Winkler, *Silence Satan: Shutting Down the Enemy's Attacks, Threats, Lies, and Accusations* (Lake Mary, FL: Charisma House, 2014).

2.   Robert L. Thomas, *New American Standard Hebrew-Aramaic and Greek Dictionaries: Updated Edition* (Anaheim: Foundation Publications, 1998).

3.   James Swanson, *Dictionary of Biblical Languages With Semantic Domains: Greek (New Testament)* (Oak Harbor: Logos Research Systems, 1997).

CHAPTER 20: "IT IS FINISHED"

1.   Robert L. Thomas, *New American Standard Hebrew-Aramaic and Greek Dictionaries: Updated Edition* (Anaheim: Foundation Publications, 1998).

2.   Michael Brown, "What Did Jesus Mean by 'It Is Finished'?" Christian Post, March 26, 2016, accessed August 30, 2016, www .christianpost.com/news/what-did-jesus-mean-by-it-is-finished-easter -resurrection-cross-160101/.

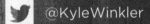

CONNECT WITH US!

CHARISMA HOUSE

(Spiritual Growth)

[f] **Facebook.com/CharismaHouse**

[t] **@CharismaHouse**

[o] **Instagram.com/CharismaHouse**

SILOAM

(Health)

[p] **Pinterest.com/CharismaHouse**

MEV MODERN ENGLISH VERSION

(Bible)
www.mevbible.com